HARVARD COLLEGE CHARGING SLIPS
(*ca.* 1823-1825)

RALPH WALDO EMERSON'S READING

A Guide for Source-Hunters and Scholars
To the One Thousand Volumes Which
He Withdrew from Libraries

Together With

SOME UNPUBLISHED LETTERS

and

A list of Emerson's contemporaries (1827-1850)—many
prominent in American Literature and in Transcendentalism—whose book borrowings are inscribed in the
charging records of the Boston Athenæum;

Also

Other Emerson Materials and an introduction describing
bibliographical resources in New England

By

Kenneth Walter Cameron

HASKELL HOUSE
Publishers of Scholarly Books
NEW YORK
1966

published by

HASKELL HOUSE

Publishers of Scholarly Books

30 East 10th Street • New York, N. Y. 10003

TO

STANLEY T. WILLIAMS

"BOOKS ARE FOR THE SCHOLAR'S IDLE TIMES.
WHEN WE CAN READ GOD DIRECTLY, THE HOUR
IS TOO PRECIOUS TO BE WASTED IN OTHER
MEN'S TRANSCRIPTS OF THEIR READINGS."
——THE AMERICAN SCHOLAR.

ACKNOWLEDGMENT

I wish to express my thanks to Dr. Henry J. Cadbury, Director, and to Dr. Jannette E. Newhall, Librarian, of the Andover-Harvard Theological Library, for permission to consult its archives, to edit a page of Emerson borrowings, and to reproduce a copy of an Emerson letter.

To the officials and staff of the Harvard College Library—in particular to Mr. Clifford K. Shipton, custodian of the Archives—I am deeply grateful for much assistance and for permission to edit the Emerson borrowings and reproduce three of the charging slips in facsimile. My warmest thanks are due Messrs. Francis P. Keough and Robert W. Lovett, both members of the Archives division, whose cheerful readiness to help was ever balm to a tired scholar.

The largest part of the research was conducted in the Library of the Boston Athenæum. Miss Elinor Gregory (Mrs. Keyes De Witt Metcalf), the Librarian, and the Board of Directors granted generous privileges, including permission to edit their records. Miss Margaret Hackett and other members of the staff have helped me in matters too numerous to mention. I must, however, indicate special thanks to Miss Marjorie Lyle Crandell, Reference Librarian, for days spent in untangling some of the difficult problems presented by the records. That the Athenæum list now presents so few mysteries is largely the result of her indefatigable efforts.

Thanks finally go to my secretary, Mr. Joseph Leeper of Gastonia, North Carolina, for his accurate assistance with the card catalogue.

K. W. C.

Cambridge, Mass.
August 1, 1941.

TABLE OF CONTENTS

INTRODUCTION

The present volume is a by-product of a forthcoming study, *The Sources and Background of Ralph Waldo Emerson's "Nature,"* on which I have been at work for several years. The examination of all available loan records was obviously a necessary preliminary step in building a bibliography for that specialized study, but it occurred to me that the publication of the material on library borrowings might have value for others, especially for those who one day will thoroughly edit the essays, poems and lectures. Although I have begrudged the time required in preparing this volume for the press, I have had the pleasure of discovering dozens of possible research subjects and new bibliographical resources for them. Not only are there fresh hints for the background of many of Emerson's important works like the *American Scholar* and *Representative Men*, but the Athenæum reading records reveal new influences on Oliver Wendell Holmes, Bronson Alcott, Sampson Reed, and George Bancroft—to name only a few. I must not enumerate all the dissertation subjects, however, for that would deprive the student of the exercise of his own initiative. The record lies before him, and he may do with it what he will.

The main outlines of Emerson's acquaintance with books have long been known. We have had the lists in the published *Journals*,[1] the discussions in specialized works like those of Goddard[2] and Christy,[3] and the excellent introduction and indexes of Professor Rusk's edition of the *Letters*.[4] For the first time, however, we now have a day-by-day account of Emerson's reading over a span of more than half a century, with definite dates as guide posts. It is possible to note at a glance those books which he used again and again, others that were withdrawn from more

---

[1]See *The Journals of Ralph Waldo Emerson*, ed. E. W. Emerson and W. E. Forbes, (10 vols.), Boston & N. Y., 1909-1914.
[2]See Harold Clarke Goddard, *Studies in New England Transcendentalism*, New York, 1908, pp. 64-81.
[3]See Arthur Christy, *The Orient in American Transcendentalism*, New York, 1932.
[4]See R. L. Rusk, *ed., The Letters of . . . Emerson*, New York, 1939.

than one library, those which he chose for his concentrated summer reading, as well as the many from which he drank less deeply. One is amused to discover, among other revelations, that he often began reading volume two of a set before touching volume one, or plunged into the middle of a three-volume work, disregarding both ends. Other interesting reading habits will become at once apparent to anyone who will glance at the lists that follow.

Before Emerson's reading record is complete, however, one very necessary bibliographical task remains to be done, and that is the publishing of an inventory of his library, now housed in the Concord Antiquarian Society and, in part, in the old home, in Concord. Two card shelf-lists have been made at different times, one of them now available to all who will visit the Antiquarian Society during its open season, but both have proved unsatisfactory, and the Ralph Waldo Emerson Memorial Association, in the near future, plans to publish for scholars an authorized list of its holdings. Such a catalogue will necessarily lack a chronology, since it will be difficult or impossible to state definitely when the separate volumes came into Emerson's collection, but some dates will certainly appear in presentation copies and will, doubtless, be included with other information important in research. Perhaps the Association will also make available in printed form the transcripts of marginalia which now may be consulted only in Concord.

The lists appearing on the following pages are not verbatim transcripts of the loan records. The condition of the latter is such as to make mere copying valueless. The charging clerks both at Harvard and at the Athenæum would often misspell titles, omit significant words, forget names of authors or give names of editors instead, and commit mistakes in penmanship which an editor considers unholy. But by means of the shelf number (almost always given) and parallel entries throughout, and with the aid of early printed catalogues and extant shelf-lists, the achievement of what I hope represents an accurate record of Emerson's reading was not impossible. Ten or fifteen items in the consolidated list gave considerable trouble, largely because the binder's title was recorded instead of that on the title-page, but handling the books themselves finally established the identification. Among the various bibliographical aids of which I availed myself were the following:

HARVARD COLLEGE LIBRARY

(a) The Harvard Charging Lists, in large bound super-folio volumes, covering the last of the Eighteenth and most of the Nineteenth centuries. There are some unfortunate gaps, notably that between 1819 and 1825, but there are bundles of "charging slips" covering 1823-1825. (All are in the Archives; call number: UA.III.50.15.60)

(b) Several sets of shelf-lists, some dated *ca.* 1822 and *ca.* 1830, all in bad order and incomplete. There are also binders' reports and various library lists of considerable value, all of which are being carefully organized by Mr. Robert W. Lovett. (All in the Archives.)

(c) *A Catalogue of the Library of Harvard University in Cambridge, Massachusetts*
   Cambridge, 1830   (3 vols.)

(d) The first supplement to the above: Cambridge, 1834.

(e) An old card catalogue, apparently the first in the United States, begun about 1850 and now discarded. It is kept in the basement of the library. The old cards are nearly nine inches long and three high and contain much information of value to the bibliographer, especially early accession dates. This catalogue was originally used only by the library staff and is in rather good condition, but now exceedingly difficult of access.

(f) Miscellaneous:

   (1) *Catalogus librorum in Bibliotheca Cantabrigiensi selectus*, Bostoniæ, 1773.

   (2) *Catalogus Bibliothecæ Harvardianæ*, Bostoniæ, 1790.

   (3) *Catalogue of Surplus Copies from the Library of Harvard University sold at auction*, [Boston, 1815].

   (4) *Catalogue of Duplicates in the Library of Harvard University for sale*, [Cambridge, 1824].

   (5) *Catalogue of Duplicates etc.*, [n.p., 1833].

HARVARD DIVINITY SCHOOL
(the library of which is known as
"The Andover-Harvard Theological Library")

(The first books in use at the Harvard Divinity School came from the college collection, apparently after 1825. The earliest loan records of the school itself begin in 1827 and continue to the middle of the century. There are a few late inventories or records of accessions, but no shelf-lists for the early period seem to have survived.)

BOSTON ATHENÆUM LIBRARY

(a) A series of 26 super-folio volumes of charging lists, covering the years 1827 through 1872. [See also (j) below.]

> (Emerson apparently drew books from the Athenæum before 1827, but the records apparently are lost.)

(b) *Catalogue of the Boston Athenæum,* [Boston, 1810].

(1) Printed copy ($XL5.B65.tr.)

(2) Manuscript copy (a folio volume containing earliest shelf or accession numbers) (B.A. C1810)

(3) Printed copy with marginal additions in handwriting. (B.A. C1810.2)

(c) *Catalogue of Books in the Boston Athenæum,* ˋBoston, 1827. (This excellent volume has the shelf-numbers of the library's first effective shelving system printed in the margins. Indispensable for interpreting the charging lists before 1840.)

(1) Many copies are available. The most valuable for the research student (:XN5.B6562.2) contains written opposite each printed number its equivalent in the second shelving system of the library. Many corrections also appear in handwriting.

(2) Supplement: *Catalogue of Books added to the Boston Athenæum since the publication of the Catalogue in January, 1827,* [Boston, 1830]. (:XN5.B6562.6)

(3) Anr. Supplement: *Catalogue of Books added to the Boston Athenæum in 1830-1833,* Boston, 1834. (:XN5 + B6562)

(4) For a large MS. supplement in four volumes, containing pages of the 1827 catalogue superimposed on large folios, with handwritten list of accessions covering the years 1827 through 1840, see (B.A. W1840). These MSS. were not, however, the basis for the following supplement, covering the same period:

(d) *Catalogue of Books added to the Boston Athenæum since the publication of the Catalogue in January, 1827,* Boston, 1840

(1) As printed. (:XN5.B6562.3)

(2) Interleaved copy with additions (B.A. C1840.2)

(e) *Catalogue of the Library of the Boston Athenæum, 1807-1871,* Boston, 1874-1880 [1882] (4, sometimes 5, volumes)

> [Among others, the Athenæum has two uncatalogued sets of this publication, each letter bound separately, with marginal call numbers of the current system inscribed in the margins. (See revolving dictionary stand near the card catalogue.) This printed catalogue was hastily compiled and contains many errors. Several important references were inadvertently omitted.]

(f) *The Influence and History of the Boston Athenæum from 1807 to 1907, with a record of its officers etc.,* [Boston], 1907.

(g) Shelf Lists:

    (1) *Shelf Catalogue (1849):* A manuscript shelf-list in two quarto volumes, containing the first permanent set of shelf numbers used by the Athenæum. There are a few gaps, but not too many to impair its great usefulness. (B.A. + WS1849) Because numbers were frequently shifted in the early period, one will need to consult the volume cited in (c) (1) above.

    (2) Shelf List (*ca.* 1850-1870) in about ninety parts, covering the system in use after the middle of the century and before the present one was established by Charles A. Cutter. These parts include books with numbers from "1" to approximately "135" and books with letters "A" through "Z." Some appear to be missing.

(h) Volumes of Accessions and Donations (Incomplete and unaccessioned.)

    (1) Accessions ("Vol. II") (5 Nov. 1827—3 May 1837)

    (2) Accessions ("Vol. III") (5 May 1837—6 Dec. 1848) (Contain occasional references to Emerson's gifts. *E.g.*, see "II", folios 396-397.)

(i) "Books Received" (1811-1849) (Apparently a record kept of the contents of packages as opened at the library.) (B.A. W1811-1849)

(j) Double-check Journals of book loans (29 May 1851—12 May 1856) (8 vols.) In addition to the charging lists mentioned in (a), the Athenæum for many years kept a journal of daily charges. Emerson's borrowings are duplicated in them for the period indicated. The "Double-check" is valuable for confirming his reading record and for indicating quickly the names of all who used the library on any particular day of the year.

(k) Miscellaneous:

    (1) Manuscript catalogue of Tracts in the Library: a scientific and alphabetical index, compiled in 1831. (4 vols.) It is valuable because the 1827 catalogue omitted all tracts, and needs to be supplemented in this particular. (B.A. || Wt)

    (2) Several small catalogues of additions, each covering only a single year. (See card catalogue.)

    (3) Catalogues of duplicates sold. (See card catalogue.)

If Emerson used the Boston Public Library after it opened its doors in 1854, no evidence survives in the form of library charging lists. The Massachusetts Historical Society, moreover, whose loan records cover most of the century, reports that Emerson's name does not appear in them.[5] The fact that most of his book borrowing occurred at the Athenæum is fortunate for scholarship, because there the annual subscription fee and the consequent limited circulation and strigent rules have resulted in the survival of most of the volumes which he used.

---

[5]Letter received from Mr. Allyn B. Forbes under date of May 26, 1941.

In concluding these introductory remarks I should like to make a few practical suggestions to the young research student. Scholars living at a distance from Boston may usually avail themselves of the courtesy extended by the Athenæum and have records or books typed or photostated at reasonable rates. For the contents of many of the sets of complete works listed in my bibliography, the latest printed catalogues of the Boston Athenæum or of the Boston Public Library (to be found in most university libraries) will give convenient analyses. The cross-reference index has been compiled for this volume because Emerson was often careless in identifying books and because an editor of his writings needs a subject guide to help him.[6] I have repeated the author's full name with each listing in order that, each item being independent, the scholar may, if he wishes, cut up the bibliography and mount it on 3 x 5 cards for use in his own way. The utility of the whole as it stands, however, will be readily apparent: the margins will provide sufficient space for the addition of local catalogue numbers and other data.

---

[6] A helpful index-concordance to key-words and ideas in Emerson appears as an appendix to my edition of *Ralph Waldo Emerson's "Nature" (1836)*, New York, 1940.

BOSTON ATHENÆUM

1 8 3 0

Jan.	1	Coleridge, *Sibylline Leaves*	Jan.	11
Jan.	1	Gerando, *Histoire Comparée* (1)	Feb.	1
Jan.	1	Wakefield, *Correspondence with C. J. Fox*	Jan.	9
Jan.	9	Aristophanes, *[Comœdiæ]*	Jan.	11
Jan.	11	Spence, *Anecdotes*	Feb.	1
Jan.	11	Parry, *Journal of a Second Voyage*	July	28
Feb.	1	Gerando, *Histoire Comparée* (2)	Mar.	1
Feb.	1	Parry, *Journal of a Third Voyage*	Feb.	18
Feb.	12	*Quarterly Review* (34)	Feb.	18
Feb.	18	Beechey, *Proceedings of the Expedition*	Mar.	4
Feb.	18	Donne, *Five Sermons*	Feb.	23
Feb.	23	Selden, *Table Talk*	Mar.	1
Mar.	4	Savage, *Compleat History of Germany*	Apr.	1
Apr.	13	Howell, *Epistolæ Ho-Elianæ*	May	12
Apr.	15	Emerson, *An Historical Sketch*	May	12
June	15	Bigelow, *Florula Bostoniensis*	July	15
June	18	Bigelow, *American Medical Botany* (2, 3)	June	23
June	23	Rees, *Cyclopædia* (1st Am. ed.) (16)	July	15
July	[15]	Kirby, *Introd. to Entomology* (1, 2)	July	23
July	30	Kirby, *Introd. to Entomology* (3)	Aug.	20
Sept.	14	Hartley, *Observations on Man* (2)	Nov.	5
Oct.	19	Kirby, *Introd. to Entomology* (1)	Nov.	19
Nov.	6	Mass. Comm[onwealth?] 182[?]	*Jan.	1
Nov.	6	Lewis, *Tales of Wonder* (1)	Nov.	12
Nov.	12	Penn, *Select Works* (1)	Nov.	19
Nov.	19	Penn, *Select Works* (2)	*Jan.	1
Nov.	19	More, *Divine Dialogues*	Dec.	9
Nov.	24	Baxter, *Treatise of Knowledge and Love*	Dec.	9
[Dec.]	9	Plato, *Works of Plato* (1)	Dec.	24
[Dec.]	24	Plato, *Works of Plato* (3)	*Jan.	1
[Dec.]	28	Browne, *Tracts*	*Jan.	1

---

* The asterisk indicates that the date belongs to the following year. Arabic numerals in parentheses refer to numbers of the volumes which Emerson withdrew; roman numerals designate the number of the series. I have included dates on which Emerson paid his annual subscription fee only when they fall on days when he did not withdraw books.

1 8 3 1

Jan.	3	Harrington, *Oceana*	Jan.	10
Jan.	4	Plato, *Works of Plato* (2, 3)	Mar.	7
Jan.	8	Paley, *View of Evidences*	Feb.	3
Jan.	18	Lardner, *Works* (1)	Mar.	15
Jan.	25	Lardner, *Works* (2)	Mar.	18
Mar.	7	Cave, *Apostolici* (1)	Mar.	25
Mar.	7	Eusebius, *Auncient Ecclesiasticall Histories*	Apr.	6
Mar.	22	Bible: *Harmony of the Gospels* (Macknight)	Apr.	31
Mar.	22	Bible: *New Literal Tr. of Epistles* (Macknight)	Apr.	24
Mar.	24	Fabricius, *Bibliotheca Græca* (4)	Apr.	29
Mar.	25	Plato, *Works of Plato* (3)	Apr.	29
Apr.	1	Browne, *Religio Medici*	May	10
Apr.	6	Gerando, *Histoire Comparée* (1)	Apr.	15
Apr.	15	*Edinburgh Review* (27)	May	3
Apr.	29	Anderson, *Works of the British Poets* (3)	May	3
Apr.	29	Schiller, *Wallenstein* (tr. Coleridge)	May	11
May	3	Herder, *Outlines of a Philosophy of Man* (1)	May	6
May	3	Southey, *Book of the Church* (1)	May	10
May	28	Schiller, *Wallenstein* (tr. Coleridge)	June	25
May	28	Kirby, *Introd. to Entomology* (1)	June	20
June	20	Scott, *The Christian Life* (1, 2)	July	7
June	25	Smith, *Christian Religion's Appeal*	July	30
July	7	Mosheim, *An Ecclesiastical History* (1)	Sept.	9
July	7	Russell, *Hist. of Modern Europe* (3)	July	20
July	30	Wilson, *Memoirs of . . . Daniel DeFoe* (1)	Aug.	29
Aug.	1	Herder, *Outlines of a Philosophy of Man* (1, 2)	Aug.	26
Aug.	11	*Edinburgh Encyclopædia* (2)	Aug.	29
Aug.	27	Landor, *Imaginary Conversations* (2nd ed.)	Sept.	9
Sept.	2	Taylor, *Works* (5, 8)	Nov.	22
Sept.	20	Cicero, *Opera* (3)	Nov.	22
Oct.	12	*Edinburgh Review* (52)	Dec.	21
Nov.	22	Hoyt, *Antiquarian Researches*	Dec.	21
Dec.	21	Taylor, *Works* (1, 15)	*Jan.	3
Dec.	23	Mueller, *Hist. and Antiq. of Doric Race* (1)	*Jan.	3

1 8 3 2

Jan.	14	Campbell, *Specimens of the British Poets* (1, 2)	Feb.	2
Jan.	14	Taylor, *Works* (4, 7)	Feb.	2

1 8 3 2			1 8 3 2
Feb.	2	Temminck, *Manuel d'Ornithologie* (1)	Feb. 10
Feb.	2	White, *Natural History of Selborne* (1, 2)	Mar. 17
Feb.	7	Knapp, *Journal of a Naturalist*	May 30
Feb.	10	Lardner, *Cabinet Cyclopædia* (19)	Feb. 15
Feb.	18	Davy, *Salmonia*	Mar. 7
Mar.	9	*Westminster Review* (6)	Mar. 17
Mar.	17	Hartley, *Observations on Man* (3)	Mar. 19
Mar.	19	Hartley, *Observations on Man* (2)	Apr. 10
Mar.	21	Hartley, *Observations on Man* (1)	Mar. 23
Mar.	21	Nitsch, *Gen'l and Introd. View* (1)	Apr. 3
Mar.	23	Biber, *Henry Pestalozzi*	May 8
Mar.	30	Hartley, *Observations on Man* (3)	May 18
Apr.	3	*Elements of Chemistry . . . explained*	Apr. 6
Apr.	10	Davy, *Elements of Agricultural Chemistry* (1)	Apr. 24
Apr.	10	Royal Soc., *Philosophical Transac. for . . . 1816*	Apr. 18
Apr.	18	Royal Soc., *Philosophical Transac. for . . . 1813*	Apr. 24
Apr.	18	Paris [France]: *Histoire de l'Académie etc.* (36)	Apr. 18
Apr.	18	Paris [France]: *Histoire de l'Académie etc.* (37)	May 8
Apr.	24	Cappe, *Critical Remarks on . . . Scripture* (1)	May 8
Apr.	24	Bryant, *Sentiments of Philo Judæus*	May 8
May	24	Leslie, *Elements of Natural Philosophy*	May 26
May	24	Mawe, *Linnean System of Conchology*	May 26
May	24	Drummond, *Letters to a Young Naturalist*	May 26
June	6	*Encyclopædia Britannica* (3)	July 21
June	6	Huber, *New Observations on . . . Bees*	June 7
June	11	Clarkson, *Portraiture of Quakerism* (1)	June 11
June	11	Penn, *Select Works* (5)	Sept. 20
June	11	Clarkson, *Portraiture of Quakerism* (2)	[July] 2
July	21	Huber, *Natural History of Ants*	July 21
July	24	*Annual Register* (of London) (58)	July 27
July	24	*Federalist* (1)	July 27
Aug.	13	North, *Lives of Francis North etc.* (1)	Aug. 20
Aug.	13	Goethe, *Wilhelm Meister's Apprenticeship* (1)	Aug. 16
Aug.	16	Goethe, *Wilhelm Meister's Apprenticeship* (2)	Aug. 23
Aug.	20	Goethe, *Memoirs*	Sept. 5
Aug.	31	*Tracts:* B 781 [Analyzed in Bibliography]	Sept. 11
Sept.	11	Sully, *Memoirs* (tr. Lennox) (5)	Oct. 13
Sept.	12	Landor, *Imaginary Conversations* (2nd. ed.) (3)	Oct. 6

1 8 3 2		1 8 3 2
Sept. 20	Hall, *Fragments of Voyages* (II.2)	Oct. 2
Sept. 20	Hall, *Fragments of Voyages* (II.3)	Oct. 2
Oct. 2	Landor, *Imaginary Conversations* (II.1)	Oct. 6
Oct. 2	Hall, *Fragments of Voyages* (I.3)	Oct. 5
Oct. 5	Lucas, *Practical Christianity*	Oct. 23
Oct. 6	Landor, *Imaginary Conversations* (2nd. ed.) (2)	Oct. 9
Oct. 6	Southey, *Essays Moral and Political* (2)	Oct. 9
Oct. 9	Hall, *Fragments of Voyages* (II.1)	Oct. 12
Oct. 12	Landor, *Imaginary Conversations* (2)	Oct. 22
Oct. 13	*New Monthly Magazine* (28)	Oct. 12
Oct. 15	*New Monthly Magazine* (29)	Oct. 27
Oct. 15	*Fraser's Magazine* (3)	Nov. 5
Oct. 23	*Blackwood's Edinburgh Magazine* (29)	Nov. 3
Oct. 27	*Fraser's Magazine* (2)	Nov. 8
Nov. 3	*Fraser's Magazine* (1)	Nov. 7
Nov. 5	Lamb, *Works*	Nov. 16
Nov. 7	*Fraser's Magazine* (4)	Nov. 10
Nov. 8	*Foreign Review* (2)	Nov. 16
Nov. 10	*Foreign Review* (1)	Nov. 17
Nov. 16	*Foreign Review* (3?)	Dec. 12
Nov. 17	Douce, *Illustrations of Shakespeare* (1, 2)	Nov. 21
Nov. 21	Baillie, *Series of Plays* (1)	Dec. 7
Dec. 3	Raynal, *A Philos. . . . Hist. of the Indies* (5)	Dec. 4
Dec. 4	Southey, *Chronological Hist. of West Indies* (1)	Dec. 5
Dec. 5	[?Russell], *History of America* (1, 2)	Dec. 5
Dec. 5	Edwards, *History . . . of . . . West Indies* (1, 2)	Dec. 12
Dec. 6	Jefferys, *Descrip. of the Spanish Islands*	Dec. 7
Dec. 6	Raynal, *A Philos. . . . Hist. of the Indies* (5)	Dec. 7
Dec. 7	Acosta, *Hist. of Spanish West Indies* (1)	Dec. 12
Dec. 7	Baillie, *Series of Plays* (2)	*Jan. 4
Dec. 12	Raynal, *A Philos. . . . Hist. of the Indies* (4, 5)	Dec. 14
Dec. 15	Paris, *Life of Sir Humphrey Davy*	*Jan. 4

1 8 3 4

Jan. 8	Royal Soc., *Philosophical Transac. for 1822*	Jan. 24
Jan. 8	*Family Library* (33)	Jan. 10
Jan. 8	Lardner, *Cabinet Cyclopædia* (17, 34)	Jan. 18
Jan. 10	Playfair, *Works* (1)	Jan. 18

1 8 3 4			1 8 3 4
Jan.	11	Wells, *Essay on Dew*	Jan. 18
Jan.	22	Bower, *Life of Luther*	Feb. 22
Feb.	20	Austin, *Characteristics of Goethe* (3)	Feb. 22
Feb.	20	Austin, *Characteristics of Goethe* (1, 2)	Apr. 17
Feb.	22	Mayo, *Memoir of Pestalozzi*	Mar. 21
Feb.	24	Bell, *Observations on Italy*	Feb. 26
Mar.	8	*Foreign Review* (2)	Apr. 8
Mar.	21	Scott, *Minstrelsy of Scottish Border* (1)	Mar. 21
Apr.	8	Wieland, *Sämmtliche Werke* (5-6, 21-22)	Apr. 9
Apr.	9	Wieland, *Sämmtliche Werke* (13-14, 17-18)	Apr. 9
Apr.	14	Scoresby, *An Acc't of Arctic Regions* (1)	Apr. 23
Apr.	[14]	Candolle, *Elements of Philos. of Plants*	May 17
Apr.	23	Wieland, *Sämmtliche Werke* (11-12)	Apr. 25
July	5	Stael-Holstein, *Œuvres Complètes* (8)	Sept. 25
July	10	Stael-Holstein, *Œuvres Complètes* (6)	July 12
July	12	Stael-Holstein, *Œuvres Complètes* (7)	July 19
Sept.	4	Jay, *Life of John Jay* (1)	Nov. 10
Sept.	4	Jay, *Life of John Jay* (2)	Oct. 18
Sept.	25	*Retrospective Review* (13)	Oct. 14
Oct.	12	*London Jour. of Arts, Sciences &c.* (III.2)	Oct. 18
Oct.	14	Coleridge, *On Constitution of Ch. and State*	*Jan. 5
Oct.	18	*London Jour. of Arts, Sciences &c.* (III.4)	Nov. 22
Oct.	18	Stanley, *History of Philosophy*	Nov. 24
Nov.	12	Bower, *Life of Luther*	Dec. 11
Nov.	22	*London Jour. of Arts. Sciences &c.* (? II.8)	*Jan. 31
Nov.	25	Luther, *Commentary upon Galatians*	Dec. 11
Dec.	11	*Fraser's Magazine* (2)	*Jan. 5
Dec.	13	*Biographie Universelle* (6)	Dec. 13
Dec.	13	Duppa, *Life of Michael Angelo*	*Jan. 12

1 8 3 5

Jan.	1	(Rec'd Subscription for 1835)	
Jan.	5	*Retrospective Review* (13)	Feb. 12
Jan.	5	Mayo, *Memoir of Pestalozzi*	Feb. 12
Jan.	19	Bower, *Life of Luther*	Feb. 20
Jan.	19	Milner, *History of the Church* (4)	Feb. 12
Feb.	12	Milton, *Prose Works with Life* (1, 3, 7)	Feb. 20
Feb.	20	Fox, *New England Fire Brand Quenched*	Mar. 15

1 8 3 5			1 8 3 5	
Feb.	20	Penn, *Select Works* (1)	Mar.	15
Feb.	20	Moore, *Memoirs of . . . Sheridan*	Apr.	1
Feb.	20	Barclay, *Apology for True Christian Divinity*	Mar.	15
Mar.	15	Austin, *Characteristics of Goethe* (1)	May	4
Mar.	15	British Ass'n, *Report of the Third Meeting*	Apr.	1
Apr.	1	Austin, *Characteristics of Goethe* (3)	May	8
Apr.	6	British Ass'n, *Report of the Third Meeting*	Apr.	27
May	28	Goethe, *Memoirs*	July	22
May	28	*Foreign Review* (1)	June	23
May	28	Schlegel, *Sämmtliche Werke* (1)	June	23
May	28	Wieland, *Sämmtliche Werke* (9)	July	22
June	23	Southey, *Hist. of Peninsula War* (1)	July	6
June	23	Lamb, *Elia* [?*First* or *Last Essays*]	July	22
July	6	Southey, *Hist. of Peninsula War* (2)	July	28
July	22	Warton, *Hist. of English Poetry*	Dec.	10
July	28	Southey, *Hist. of Peninsula War* (3)	Aug.	12
Aug.	12	Southey, *Hist. of Peninsula War* (4)	Sept.	23
Sept.	3	Hutchinson, *Collection of Orig. Papers*	Oct.	7
Sept.	3	Bulkley, *The Gospel-covenant*	Oct.	7
Oct.	[20]	Turner, *Hist. of the Anglo-Saxons* (1, 2)	Nov.	19
Nov.	19	Shakespeare, *Plays and Poems* (Malone) (2)	Dec.	18
Nov.	[19]	Burnett, *Specimens of Eng. Prose Writers* (1)	Dec.	10
Dec.	10	Shakespeare, *Plays and Poems* (Malone) (3)	Dec.	18
Dec.	10	Hartley, *Observations on Man* (1, 2)	*Feb.	1
Dec.	18	Landor, *Imaginary Conversations* (II.1, 2)	*Jan.	15

1 8 3 6

Jan.	1	(Rec'd Subscription for 1836)		
Feb.	2	Hallam, *View of State of Europe* (2)	Feb.	25
Feb.	2	Pückler-Muskau, *Tour in England etc.*	Mar.	1
Feb.	3	Ross, *Narrative of a Second Voyage*	Feb.	25
Feb.	10	Dante, *Vision of Hell etc.* (tr. Cary) (3)	Mar.	21
Feb.	15	Bartram, *Travels*	Feb.	16
Feb.	16	Confucius, *Works* (Marshman)	Mar.	1
Feb.	25	Milton, *Prose Works with Life* (5)	Apr.	4
Mar.	17	Candole, *Elements of Philos. of Plants*	May	10
Mar.	21	Avesta, *Zend-avesta de Zoroastre* (2)	Apr.	4
Apr.	5	Sophocles [*Tragoediæ Septem*] (2)	May	2

1 8 3 6			1 8 3 6	
Apr.	5	Grimm, *Kinder- und Haus-Märchen* (3)	Apr.	21
Apr.	21	Musaeus, *Volksmärchen der Deutschen* (1, 5)	Apr.	28
July	7	Bell, *Essays on Anatomy of Expression*	Aug.	26
Aug.	2	Plato, *Works of Plato* (4)	Nov.	28
Aug.	2	Hardenberg, *Schriften*	Oct.	10
Aug.	22	Biber, *Henry Pestalozzi*	Oct.	3
Oct.	4	Lyell, *Principles of Geology* (1, 2)	Oct.	29
Oct.	10	Southey, *Book of the Church* (1, 2)	Oct.	29
Nov.	18	*Annual Register* (for 1835)	Dec.	15
Nov.	18	Aristophanes, *Comedies* (tr. Mitchell) (1)	Nov.	28
Nov.	18	Aristotle, *Ethics and Politics* (tr. Gillies) (1, 2)	Nov.	20

1 8 3 7

Jan.	2	(Rec'd Subscription for 1837)		
Jan.	6	Turner, *Hist. of the Anglo-Saxons* (1)	Jan.	27
Jan.	27	Turner, *Hist. of the Anglo-Saxons* (2)	Feb.	22
Feb.	22	Ariosto, *Orlando Furioso* (tr. Rose) (3)	Feb.	24
Feb.	22	Strutt, *Queenhoo Hall* (1)	Feb.	22
Feb.	22	Strutt, *Chronicles of England* (1)	Feb.	23
Feb.	23	Strutt, *Chronicles of England* (2)	Mar.	23
Mar.	7	Wieland, *Sämmtliche Werke* (21)	Mar.	8
Mar.	8	Wieland, *Sämmtliche Werke* (43-44)	Mar.	20
Mar.	24	Austin, *Characteristics of Goethe* (1)	May[20?]	
Mar.	24	Jacobi, *Werke* (2)	Apr.	24
Mar.	24	Ginguené, *Histoire Littéraire d'Italie* (1, 2)	Apr.	24
Apr.	24	Austin, *Characteristics of Goethe* (2)	May	10
May	29	Audubon, *Ornithological Biography* (1)	July	25
May	29	Wilson and Bonaparte, *Am. Ornithology* (1, 2, 3)	Sept.	9
Oct.	10	Chateaubriand, *Sketches of Eng. Lit.* (1)	Oct.	24
Oct.	10	Æschylus, *Tragedies* (tr. Potter)	Nov.	10
Oct.	11	Lardner, *Cabinet Cyclopædia* (84, 91)	Oct.	24
Oct.	24	Lardner, *Cabinet Cyclopædia* (71)	Nov.	10
Nov.	10	*The Examiner* (of London) (Sept. 17, 1837)	*Feb.	8
Dec.	14	Lardner, *Cabinet Cyclopædia* (2, 93)	*Feb.	8
Dec.	14	Turner, *Hist. of the Anglo-Saxons* (1, 2)	*Feb.	21
Dec.	28	Sophocles, *Tragedies* (tr. Potter)	*Feb.	14

1 8 3 8

Jan.	25	(Rec'd Subscription for 1838)		
Feb.	15	*Foreign Quarterly Review* (10)	May	9
Mar.	1	*Fraser's Magazine* (2, 5)	May	9
Mar.	1	*Foreign Quarterly Review* (8)	May	9
Mar.	1	*Fraser's Magazine* (8)	May	9
May	23	*Fraser's Magazine* (2, 3)	June	23
June	20	*Foreign Quarterly Review* (8)	July	7
June	30	Lardner, *Cabinet Cyclopædia* (80, 93, 99)	Oct.	1
June	30	Shakespeare, *Plays and Poems* (Malone) (20)	Oct.	1
Oct.	2	Belzoni, *Narrative of the Operations* (1, 2)	Nov.	19
Oct.	2	Pepys, *Memoirs* (1)	Oct.	22
Nov.	9	Pepys, *Memoirs* (2)	*Jan.	10
Nov.	22	Spence, *Anecdotes*	*Jan.	10
Nov.	22	Southey, *The Doctor &c.* (3)	Dec.	27
Dec.	27	*Fraser's Magazine* (?6, 7)	*Apr.	3

1 8 3 9

Jan.	1	(Rec'd Subscription for 1839)		
Jan.	10	*Fraser's Magazine* (8)	Apr.	16
Jan.	17	Plato, *Works of Plato* (3)	Apr.	19
Mar.	16	*Fraser's Magazine* (11)	Apr.	16
Apr.	3	*Fraser's Magazine* (15)	May	8
Apr.	19	Stael-Holstein, *Corinna; or Italy* (1, 2)	May	8
May	23	*Fraser's Magazine* (2)	June	25
May	23	*Fraser's Magazine* (6)	June	25
Sept.	20	White, *Natural Hist. of Selborne* (1)	Nov.	1
Sept.	20	Lardner, *Cabinet Cyclopædia* (63, 96, 108)	Oct.	5
Oct.	14	Lardner, *Cabinet Cyclopædia* (101)	Nov.	1
Oct.	14	Lardner, *Cabinet Cyclopædia* (115)	Nov.	1
Oct.	14	White, *Natural Hist. of Selborne* (2)	Nov.	8
Nov.	1	Linnæus, *Lachesis Lapponica*	Dec.	12
Nov.	[1]	*Harleian Miscellany* (4)	*Jan.	9
Nov.	[1]	Lardner, *Cabinet Cyclopædia* (112)	Dec.	12
Dec.	12	Hazlitt, *Literary Remains* (1, 2)	*Jan.	30
Dec.	12	Hallam, *Introd. to Lit. of Europe* (4)	*Feb.	6

1 8 4 0

Jan.	4	Grenville, *Memorials of J. Hampden* (1)	Jan.	30
Jan.	[?]	Grenville, *Memorials of J. Hampden* (2)	May	27
Jan.	30	Beyle, *Lives of Haydn and Mozart*	Apr.	23
Feb.	4	Michaux, *Histoire des Chênes*	Feb.	4
Feb.	18	Hamilton [*Memoirs* or *Memoires*] (1, 2)	Apr.	23
July	23	Jones (Wm.), *Works* (3)	Sept.	22
July	23	Spenser, *Works* (5)	Sept.	22
July	23	Rabelais, *Œuvres* (1, 2)	Sept.	22
Sept.	22	Ockley, *Conquest of Syria* (1, 2)	Dec.	12
Nov.	18	Bryant, *Analysis of Ancient Mythology* (1)	*Feb.	17
....	..	Mignan, *Travels in Chaldæa*	Dec.	31
....	..	Junot, *Memoirs* [in English] (3)	Dec.	24
....	..	Burnet, *History of His Own Time* (1)	Dec.	31
....	..	Junot, *Memoirs* [in English] (4)	Dec.	31
....	..	Junot, *Memoirs* [in English] (5)	*Feb.	8

1 8 4 2

Jan.	1	(Rec'd Subscription for 1842)		
....	..	Junot, *Memoirs* [in English] (6, 7, 8)	Feb.	25
Feb.	8	Corneille, *The Cid*	Mar.	26
Feb.	18	Percy, *Reliques of Ancient Eng. Poetry* (2, 3)	May	11
Apr.	27	Plato, *Works of Plato* (5)	May	11
Apr.	27	Beaumont and Fletcher, *Dramatick Works* (3)	May	11
May	26	*Philosophical Magazine* (of London) (19)	July	26
May	26	Waagen, *Works of Art and Artists of Eng.* (1, 2)	Aug.	4
June	28	Waagen, *Works of Art and Artists of Eng.* (3)	July	26
July	26	Sidney, *Works* (1, 2, 3)	Aug.	11
July	26	Lytton, *Ernest Maltravers* (1, 2)	Oct.	6
Aug.	11	Lytton, *Alice; or the Mysteries* (1, 2)	Oct.	6
Aug.	25	Tytler, *Life of Sir Walter Raleigh*	Nov.	23
Oct.	7	Raleigh, *History of the World*	Nov.	23
Oct.	25	Ockley, *Conquest of Syria* (2)	Oct.	5
Dec.	27	Chevalier, *Society, Manners &c. in U. S.*	*May	11

1 8 4 5

Jan.	1	Fauvelet, *Private Memoirs of Napoleon* (1, 2)	Jan.	8
Jan.	1	Antommarchi, *Last Days of Napoleon* (1)	Jan.	8
Jan.	1	Caulincourt, *Recollections of Caulincourt* (1)	Jan.	8

1 8 4 5			1 8 4 5	
Jan.	8	Fauvelet, *Private Memoirs of Napoleon* (3, 4)	Jan.	16
Jan.	8	Caulincourt, *Recollections of Caulincourt* (2)	Jan.	16
Jan.	8	Napoleon I., *Memoirs of the Hist. of France* (1)	Jan.	16
Jan.	16	*Family Library* (1, 8)	Jan.	30
Jan.	16	Russell, *Life of Cromwell* (1)	Jan.	30
Jan.	16	Bausset, *Private Memoirs of Court of Napoleon*	Feb.	11
Jan.	..	Fouché, *Memoirs*	Feb.	11
Jan.	..	Villemarest, *Life of Prince Talleyrand* (1, 2)	Feb.	11
Feb.	11	Villemarest, *Life of Prince Talleyrand* (3, 4)	Feb.	18
Feb.	13	Beckford, *Italy . . . Spain and Portugal* (1, 2)	Feb.	24
Feb.	19	Ducrest, *Memoirs of Empress Josephine* (1)	Mar.	12
Mar.	6	Wieland, *Sämmtliche Werke* (7-8)	Mar.	12
Mar.	7	Literary and Philos. Soc. of N. Y., *Transac.* (1)	Mar.	22
Mar.	7	*Jour. of Acad. of Nat'l Sciences of Phila.* (1)	Mar.	22
Mar.	22	Percy, *Reliques of Ancient Eng. Poetry* (1, 2, 3)	May	10
Apr.	16	Wieland, *Sämmtliche Werke* (33-34)	May	10
June	2	Plato, *Works of Plato* (4)	Sept.	4
June	2	Shelley, *Essays, Letters from Abroad &c.* (1)	Sept.	4
July	7	Stael-Holstein, *Œuvres Complètes* (15)	Aug.	12
July	7	Plato, *Works of Plato* (1)	Sept.	4
Sept.	4	Landor, *Imaginary Conversations* (II.1, 2)	Sept.	29
Sept.	4	*Blackwood's Edinburgh Magazine* (50, 52)	Nov.	4
Sept.	16	D'Isræli, *Amenities of Literature* (3)	*Jan.	28
Nov.	4	Schlegel, *Lectures on Hist. of Lit.* (1, 2)	*Jan.	28

1 8 5 1

Jan.	7	Goethe, *Werke* (21)	Feb.	20
Jan.	8	[?Cobbett], *Parliamentary Debates* (5)	Feb.	20
Jan.	31	Columbus, *Select Letters*	Mar.	14
Mar.	6	Cumming, *Five Years of a Hunter's Life* (1)	Mar.	14
Mar.	6	St. John, *Hist. of Manners of Ancient Greece* (1, 3)	Mar.	14
Mar.	14	St. John, *Hist. of Manners of Ancient Greece* (2)	Apr.	21
Apr.	9	Quatremère de Quincy, *Essay on . . . Fine Arts*	May	15
Apr.	9	Britton, *Hist. . . . Cathedral Ch. of Winchester*	May	21
May	6	Campbell, *Lives of Chief Justices of Eng.* (1)	May	15
June	4	Evelyn, *Diary and Correspondence* (2)	July	8
June	4	Campbell, *Lives of Chief Justices of Eng.* (2)	Aug.	25
Sept.	12	Hardenberg, *Schriften* (1, 2)	Dec.	5

1 8 5 1		1 8 5 1
Sept. 12	Schiller, *Correspondence . . . with Körner* (2)	Sept. 25
Sept. 25	Schiller, *Correspondence betw. S. and Goethe* (2)	Oct. 30
Nov. 26	Moore, *Letters and Journal of Lord Byron* (1)	Dec. 30
Nov. 28	Ruskin, *Stones of Venice*	*Jan. 5
Dec. 6	Moore, *Letters and Journal of Lord Byron* (2)	Dec. 30

1 8 5 2

July 8	Bristed, *Five Years in an Eng. University* (2)	Aug. 23
July 8	Davies, *Mythology and Rites of British Druids*	July 17
July 17	Bristed, *Five Years in an Eng. University* (1)	Aug. 23
Aug. 13	Johnston, *England As It Is* (1, 2)	Aug. 23
Aug. 23	Taylor, *Life and Times of Peel* (1, 2)	Sept. 6
Sept. 6	Fuller, *Hist. of the Worthies of England* (1)	Sept. 11
Sept. 6	Ruskin, *Stones of Venice*	Dec. 27
Sept. 6	Medwin, *Life of Shelley* (?1)	Dec. 11
Sept. 6	Kemble, *The Saxons in England* (1)	Dec. 27
Sept. 11	Kemble, *The Saxons in England* (2)	Dec. 27
Sept. 11	Medwin, *Life of Shelley* (2)	Dec. 27
Sept. 11	Curzon, *Visits to Monasteries of the Levant*	Oct. 7
Sept. 11	Fuller, *Hist. of the Worthies of England* (2)	Oct. 27
Sept. 27	Camden, *Britannia; Britain*	Dec. 23
Sept. 27	Luther, *Life written by Himself* (ed. Michelet)	Dec. 16
Sept. 27	Jesse, *George Selwyn and Contemporaries* (1)	Oct. 7
Oct. 7	Jesse, *George Selwyn and Contemporaries* (2)	Oct. 18
Oct. 7	Bell, *British Theatre* (29)	Oct. 28
Oct. 7	Sheridan, *Works* (2)	Oct. 16
Oct. 7	Cobbett, *Annual Register* [3?]	Oct. 16
Oct. 16	Cobbett, *Parliamentary Debates* (27, 28)	Oct. 23
Oct. 16	Brougham, *Speeches upon Questions* (2)	Oct. 28
Oct. 16	Jesse, *George Selwyn and Contemporaries* (3)	Oct. 23
Oct. 25	*Cobbett's Political Register* (17)	Nov. 9
Oct. 25	Voltaire, *Œuvres complètes* (61)	Dec. 23
Oct. 28	Brougham, *Speeches upon Questions* (1)	Dec. 9
Oct. 25	*Cobbett's Political Register* (17)	Nov. 9
Nov. 9	Brougham, *Speeches upon Questions* (2, 4)	Dec. 23
Nov. 9	Jesse, *George Selwyn and his Contemporaries* (4)	Dec. 23
Nov. 9	Wraxall, *Posthumous Memoirs* (1)	Dec. 23

1 8 5 3

June	13	Wraxall, *Posthumous Memoirs* (2)	July	2
June	13	Giles, *History of the Ancient Britons* (1)	July	2
June	13	Thierry, *History of the Conquest of England*	July	12
July	2	Wraxall, *Posthumous Memoirs* (3)	July	12
July	2	Henricus, *Chronicle* (Bohn ed.)	Aug.	22
Aug.	23	Porter, *The Progress of the Nation*	Oct.	21
Aug.	23	Cockburn, *Life of Lord Jeffrey* (1, 2)	Oct.	18
Sept.	24	Wraxall, *Historical Memoirs* (1)	Oct.	18
Sept.	24	Mirabeau, *Letters during Residence in Eng.* (1)	Nov.	4
Sept.	24	Mirabeau, *Letters during Residence in Eng.* (2)	Oct.	21
Oct.	18	Moore, *Memoirs, Journal and Correspondence* (2)	Oct.	22
Oct.	18	Moore, *Memoirs, Journal and Correspondence* (1, 3)	Oct.	21
Oct.	29	Moore, *Memoirs, Journal and Correspondence* (4)	Nov.	29
Nov.	4	Guizot, *History of Civilization*	*Apr.	7
Nov.	5	Southey, *Life and Correspondence* (4)	Nov.	15
Nov.	21	Grimm, *Correspondance* (II.1)	Nov.	29
Nov.	21	Macaulay, *Speeches* (1)	Dec.	20
Nov.	30	*Quarterly Review* (41)	Dec.	31
Nov.	30	[Fellows, *Travels and Researches in*] *Asia Minor*	Dec.	31
Nov.	30	Grimm, *Correspondance* (2)	Dec.	13
Dec.	13	Grimm, *Correspondance* (1.3)	Dec.	20
Dec.	20	Grimm, *Correspondance* (II.4)	Dec.	26
Dec.	26	Grimm, *Correspondance* (I.5)	*Feb.	25
Dec.	31	Sainte-Beuve, *Causeries du Lundi* (3, 4)	*Mar.	23

1 8 5 4

Jan.	16	Jones, *Attempts in Verse* (Southey)	Jan.	18
Feb.	25	Grimm, *Correspondance* (4, 5)	May	10
Mar.	23	*Revue des Deux Mondes* (Apr. 15, 1853)	Mar.	28
Mar.	24	Sainte-Beuve, *Causeries du Lundi* (5)	Apr.	20
Mar.	29	*Revue des Deux Mondes* (Mar. 1, 1853)	Apr.	7
Mar.	29	*Revue des Deux Mondes* (Jan. 1 & 15, 1854)	Apr.	7
Apr.	3	Beattie, *Life and Letters of Campbell* (3)	Apr.	7
May	10	*Revue des Deux Mondes* (Feb. 1 & 15, [1854])	May	18
July	7	Collingwood, *Selection from* [*his*] *Correspondence*	July	19
July	8	Lieber, *Manual of Political Ethics* (1, 2)	July	25
July	19	*Revue des Deux Mondes* (Jan. 1, Mar. 15, 1854)	July	26
July	19	*Revue des Deux Mondes* (Mar. 1, 1854)	Sept.	11

1 8 5 4			1 8 5 4	
July	26	Retz, [*Memoirs of the Cardinal de Retz*] (1)	Aug.	12
July	26	Dumont, *Recollections of Mirabeau*	Aug.	12
July	26	Retz, *Memoirs of the Cardinal de Retz* (1)	Aug.	14
July	26	Raumer, *England* [*in 1835*(?) *in 1841*(?)]	Aug.	12
Aug.	12	Retz, *Memoirs of the Cardinal de Retz* (2)	Sept.	11
Sept.	11	Retz, *Memoirs of the Cardinal de Retz* (3)	Oct.	20
Sept.	11	Hooker, *Ecclesiastical Politie*	*Apr.	17
Sept.	11	Pepys, *Memoirs* (1)	Oct.	25
Sept.	25	Pepys, *Memoirs* (2)	Oct.	14
Sept.	25	Evelyn, *Diary and Correspondence* (1)	Oct.	6
Sept.	25	Craik, *Sketches of the Hist. of Lit.* (1)	Oct.	6
Oct.	6	Evelyn, *Diary and Correspondence* (2)	Oct.	14
Oct.	7	Evelyn, *Diary and Correspondence* (3)	Nov.	10
Oct.	14	Sidney, *Miscellaneous Works*	Dec.	2
Oct.	14	Evelyn, *Miscellaneous Writings*	Dec.	23
Oct.	20	Homer, [*Works*] (3 Chapman translations in 1 vol.)	Dec.	5
Nov.	16	Drummond, *Notes of Ben Jonson's Conversations*	Nov.	21
Nov.	16	Romilly, *Memoirs by Himself* (1)	Nov.	21
Nov.	21	Romilly, *Memoirs by Himself* (3)	Nov.	23
Nov.	23	Sainte-Beuve, *Causeries du Lundi* (8)	Dec.	7
Dec.	1	*Maháwanso, The*	*Jan.	16
Dec.	7	*Revue des Deux Mondes* (Sept. 15, 1854)	Dec.	8
Dec.	8	Wieland, *Sämmtliche Werke* (5, 6)	Dec.	26
Dec.	11	*Revue des Deux Mondes* (August, [1854])	Dec.	20
Dec.	26	Knowles, *Life and Writings of H. Fuseli* (2, 3)	*Jan.	30

1 8 5 5

Jan.	12	Ferrier, *Destiny* (1, 2)	Feb.	13
Jan.	12	*Edinburgh Review* (36)	Apr.	11
Jan.	16	Cellini, *Memoirs* (1)	Apr.	11
Jan.	30	Dibden, *Reminiscences* (1)	May	9
Feb.	1	Niebuhr, *Life and Letters* (1)	Apr.	10
Feb.	1	Niebuhr, *Life and Letters* (2)	Apr.	11
Mar.	22	Hay [? *Principles of Beauty in Coloring*]	May	9
Apr.	11	*Blackwood's Edinburgh Magazine* (74)	May	9
Apr.	11	Niebuhr, [*Lectures on*] *History of Rome* (2)	May	4
Apr.	13	*Edinburgh Review* (22)	May	4
May	5	Vedas, *Rig-veda-sanhitá* (1, 2)	May	9

1 8 5 5		1 8 5 5	
May 26	Quarterly Review (15)	Sept.	4
May 26	Revue des Deux Mondes (Jan., Mar., 1854)	July	2
June 18	De Lolme, "On the Eng. Constitution"	Oct.	8
June 22	Digby, Private Memoirs	Aug.	14
July 2	Moore, Memoirs, Journal and Correspondence (6)	Aug.	14
July 25	Brewster, Memoirs of Sir Isaac Newton (2)	Aug.	14
July 31	Trench, The Lessons in Proverbs	Oct.	8
Aug. 14	Moore, Memoirs, Journal and Correspondence (5)	Oct.	15
Sept. 4	Montagu, Letters and Works	Oct.	8
Sept. 4	Prichard, The Natural History of Man	Oct.	8
Sept. 4	Moore, Notes from [his Suppressed] Letters	Oct.	8
Oct. 15	Waagen, Treasures of Art in Great Britain (3)	Dec.	10
Oct. 15	Madden, Literary Life and Correspondence etc. (1)	Oct.	27
Oct. 15	Madden, Literary Life and Correspondence etc. (2)	Nov.	7
Nov. 8	Edinburgh Review (99)	Dec.	10

1 8 5 6

Dec. 3	Trench, Calderon: his Life and Genius	*Mar.	12
Dec. 3	Fraser's Magazine (50)	Dec.	10
Dec. 11	Sainte-Beuve, [Causeries du Lundi] (10)	*Apr.	11
Dec. 13	Gosse, Aquarium	Dec.	29
Dec. 27	Gosse, Tenby: A Sea-side Holiday	Dec.	29

1 8 5 7

Jan. 1	(Rec'd Subscription for 1857)		
Mar. 26	Harford, Life of Michael Angelo (1)	Apr.	13
Mar. 28	Richter, Sämmtliche Werke (27, 28)	Aug.	15
Apr. 11	Harford, Life of Michael Angelo (2)	Apr.	24
May 6	Loménie, Beaumarchais and His Times (1)	June	1
May 6	Bacon, Works (ed. Spedding and Ellis) (1)	June	4
July 20	Wieland, Sämmtliche Werke (21, 22)	Aug.	7
July 20	Child, English and Scottish Ballads (1)	Aug.	24
July 20	Loménie, Beaumarchais and His Times (4)	Aug.	7
July 25	Mechanics' Magazine (Mar., Apr., 1857)	Aug.	7
Aug. 7	Loménie, Beaumarchais and His Times (3)	Aug.	15
Aug. 7	Andersen, Danish Fairy Legends and Tales	Aug.	17
Aug. 10	Barbieri, [? Etchings] [MS: "Guercino's Designs"]	Aug.	17

1 8 5 7		1 8 5 7
Aug. 10	Rosa, [? *Serie di 85 Disegni*] [MS: "Salvator Rosa's Do."]	Aug. 17
Oct. 6	Smiles, *Life of George Stephenson*	Oct. 31
Oct. 16	Payen, *Documents inédits sur Montaigne*	Oct. 31
Oct. 16	Loomis, *Recent Progress of Astronomy*	Dec. 31
Oct. 31	Arago, *Biographies of Scientific Men*	*Jan. 14
Nov. 18	Linnæus, *Lachesis Lapponica* (1, 2)	Dec. 31
Nov. 24	Pultenay, *Gen'l View of Writings of Linnæus*	*Jan. 14
Dec. 31	About, *Greece and the Greeks*	*Mar. 11
Dec. 31	*Cabala; sive, Scrinia Sacra*	*Mar. 3

1 8 5 8

Jan. 14	(Rec'd Subscription for 1858)	
Jan. 20	Bandello, *Novelle* (7, 8)	Jan. 26
Jan. 21	*Revue des Deux Mondes* (May, Sept., 1857)	Mar. 3
Feb. 1	Gurowski, *America and Europe*	Mar. 11
Apr. 1	Lockhart, *Ancient Spanish Ballads*	July 7
Apr. 17	Demosthenes, *Orations* (tr. Kennedy) (Bohn)	July 7
June 7	Wilkinson, *Modern Egypt and Thebes* (1)	July 22
June 22	Phipps, *A Year of Revolution (1848)* (1)	July 7
June 27	Phipps, *A Year of Revolution (1848)* (2)	July 22
July 7	Pulteney, *Gen'l View of Writings of Linnæus*	Aug. 12
July 7	*Revue des Deux Mondes* (Sept., Oct., 1857)	Aug. 12
Sept. 10	Hammond, *Hills, Lakes and Forest Streams*	*Aug. 15
Sept. 10	Linnæus, *Lachesis Lapponica*	Oct. 23
Sept. 10	Tautphœus, *Quits*	Oct. 23
Sept. 17	Blanc, *1848: Historical Revelations*	Oct. 23
Sept. 17	Carey, *The Past, Present and Future*	Oct. 23
Sept. 17	Carey, *Principles of Social Science* (1)	Ret'd.
Sept. 30	*Illustrated London News* (Jan.-June, 1858)	Dec. 8
Nov. 12	*Mabinogion, The* (2)	Dec. 8
Dec. 29	*Mabinogion, The* (3)	*Feb. 28

1 8 5 9

Mar. 9	(Rec'd Subscription for '59)	
Mar. 15	Grote, *History of Greece* (8)	June 18
June 25	Ruskin, *Modern Painters* (4)	Aug. 1
July 18	Diderot, *Memoires, Correspondance etc.* (4)	Aug. 1

1 8 5 9			1 8 5 9	
Aug.	1	Froude, *History of England* (1)	Aug.	15
Aug.	16	Froude, *History of England* (2)	Aug.	18
Sept.	12	Froude, *History of England* (3)	Oct.	22
Sept.	12	Hénault, *Abrégé Chronologique*	*Jan.	19
Sept.	20	Piozzi, *Anecdotes of Samuel Johnson*	Ret'd	
Oct.	8	Masson, *Essays Biographical and Critiçal*	*Jan.	19
Oct.	22	Sanders, *Das Volksleben der Neugriechen*	*Jan.	19
Oct.	22	Giles, *Life and Times of Alfred the Great*	*Jan.	19

1 8 6 0

Jan.	7	Blackwood, *Letters from High Latitudes*	Mar.	12
Mar.	31	Southey, *Common-Place Book* (2nd Ser.)	May	1
Apr.	3	Southey, *Common-Place Book* (3rd Ser.)	May	1
Apr.	16	Owen, *Palæontology*	May	1
Apr.	23	*Mabinogion, The* (1)	May	1
June	9	Oliphant, *Narrative of Elgin's Mission* (1)	Aug.	24
June	9	Owen, *Palæontology*	July	24
June	9	[? Youatt, *The Horse*]	Aug.	25
July	13	Töpffer, *Premiers Voyages en Zigzag*	Sept.	29
Aug.	15	Vedas, *Rig-veda-sanhitá* (3)	Oct.	27
Aug.	25	Malory, *Byrth of Kyng Arthur* (Southey) (1)	*Jan.	7
Aug.	25	*Revue des Deux Mondes* (May, 1860)	Sept.	7
Sept.	5	Humboldt, [*Letters to Varnhagen*]	Sept.	7
Sept.	5	Coultas, *What May Be Learned from a Tree*	*Jan.	7
Sept.	7	Malory, *Byrth of Kyng Arthur* (Southey) (2)	*Jan.	7
Sept.	7	Sainte-Beuve, [*Nouveaux Lundis*] (1)	Oct.	27
Oct.	27	Snorri, *Heimskringla* (Laing) (3)	Oct.	27
Nov.	5	*Westminster Review* (50)	*Jan.	7
Dec.	18	Rogers, *Recollections of Table Talk*	*Jan.	7
Dec.	21	Rogers, *Recollections*	*Feb.	19

1 8 6 1

Jan.	21	(Rec'd Subscription for 1861)		
Jan.	26	Whitehead, *Wild Sports of the South*	Feb.	4
Feb.	4	*Bibliotheca Indica*	May	2
Feb.	4	Jalal-ad-Din, *Auswahl aus den Diwanen*	Feb.	28
Feb.	4	Forbes, *Occasional Papers on Glaciers*	Feb.	19
Feb.	4	McClintock, *Voyage of the "Fox"*	Feb.	19

1 8 6 1			1 8 6 1	
Feb.	19	*Mabinogion, The* (1)	Mar.	30
Feb.	19	Cochrane, *Autobiography of a Seaman* (1)	Feb.	28
Feb.	21	Goethe, *Theory of Colours* (Eastlake)	June	5
Feb.	28	Southey, *Common-Place Book* (1st Ser.)	May	25
Mar.	23	Gosse, *Letters from Alabama*	Mar.	30
Apr.	10	Warner, *Dollars and Cents*	May	9
Apr.	10	Welcker, *Alte Denkmäler Erklärt* (1)	Apr.	24
Apr.	18	Welcker, *Alte Denkmäler Erklärt* (2)	Apr.	24
Apr.	24	Argenson, *Journal et Mémoires* (1)	Apr.	27
May	9	Winthrop, *History of New England* (1, 2)	June	5
May	9	Mather, *Magnalia Christi Americani*	June	5
July	17	Broderip, *Memorials of Thomas Hood* (2)	June	26
July	17	Adams, *Lectures on Rhetoric* (2)	Aug.	9
July	26	Hood, *Prose and Verse*	Sept.	10
July	26	Boner, *Chamois Hunting in Bavaria*	Aug.	9
Aug.	19	*Njals Saga* (1)	Aug.	31
Aug.	19	Wilson, *Private Diary* (1)	Aug.	31
Aug.	27	Austen, *Pride and Prejudice*	Oct.	14
Aug.	27	Brown, *Lectures on the Atomic Theory* (1)	*May	10
Aug.	31	Wilson, *Private Diary* (2)	Sept.	10
Aug.	31	*Njals Saga* (2)	Sept.	10
Sept.	10	Mueller, *Hist. of Ancient Sanskrit Lit.*	Nov.	27
Sept.	18	Watson, *Life of Richard Porson*	Error	
Oct.	7	Roper, *Life of Sir Thos. More*	*Jan.	8
Oct.	14	Petitot, Collection des Mémoires (1)	*Mar.	7
Nov.	5	Gasparin, *Uprising of a Great People* (Booth)	Nov.	13
Dec.	30	Bradford, *History of Plymouth Plantation*	*Mar.	5
Dec.	30	Loring, *The Hundred Boston Orators*	*Jan.	2
Dec.	30	Guillim, *Display of Heraldrie*	*Feb.	22

1 8 6 2

Feb.	10	Sadi, *The Gulistan* (tr. Ross)	Feb.	11
Feb.	10	Sadi, *The Gulistan* (tr. Eastwick)	Mar.	5
Feb.	26	*Book of Costume*	Mar.	5
Feb.	26	Mueller, *Lectures on the Science of Language*	Mar.	5
Mar.	5	Hope, *Costume of the Ancients* (2)	Mar.	17
Mar.	5	"Ancient Costume" (3) [Not identified]	Mar.	17
Mar.	29	Petitot, *Collection des Mémoires* (1)	May	21

1 8 6 2		1 8 6 2
Apr. 14	Alison, *Lives of Lord Castlereagh etc.* (3)	Apr. 17
Apr. 17	Hafiz, *Eine Sammlung persischer Gedichte*	June 2
June 30	Mommsen, *History of Rome* (1)	July 7
July 14	Arnold, *On Translating Homer*	Aug. 27
Aug. 27	Dicey, *Cavour: A Memoir*	Sept. 25
Sept. 17	Thornbury, *Life of J. M. W. Turner* (1, 2)	Sept. 24
Oct. 6	Eliot, *History of Liberty* (1, 2)	Nov. 20
Oct. 6	Dudevant, *L'Homme de Neige* (2, 3)	Oct. 25
Oct. 13	Hazlitt, *Round Table*	Dec. 9
Oct. 13	Thackeray, *The Four Georges*	Dec. 9
Oct. 25	Dudevant, *Mauprat*	Oct. 27
Oct. 25	Gasparin, *Les Etats-Unis en 1861*	*Apr. 6
Oct. 27	Boislecomte, *De la Crise Americaine*	Dec. 9
Dec. 9	Arnold, *Merope, A Tragedy*	Ret'd
Dec. 9	Arnold, *On Translating Homer*	Ret'd
Dec. 17	Dudevant, *La Petite Fadette*	Ret'd

1 8 6 3

Feb. 12	Fichte, *Popular Works* (tr. Smith) (2)	Feb. 28
Feb. 16	Renan, *Essais de Morale et de Critique*	Apr. 6
Feb. 28	Borrow, *Wild Wales* (1)	Mar. 6
Mar. 5	Borrow, *Wild Wales* (2)	Mar. 11
Mar. 5	Varnhagen von Ense, *Tagebücher* (1)	Apr. 6
Mar. 10	Borrow, *Wild Wales* (3)	Mar. 18
Mar. 10	Varnhagen von Ense, *Tagebücher* (2)	Mar. 19
Apr. 6	Varnhagen von Ense, *Tagebücher* (3, 4)	[May] 15
Apr. 13	Varnhagen von Ense, *Denkwürdigkeiten* (8)	May 15
May 15	Moody, *Biog. Sketches of the Moody Family*	May 15
May 25	Montluc, *The Commentaries*	June 9
May 25	Herbert, *Life of Edward Lord Herbert*	June 9
July 24	Sainte-Beuve, *Nouveaux Lundis* (1)	Aug. 1
July 24	Murger, *Adeline Protat*	Aug. 1
Aug. 3	Sainte-Beuve, *Causeries du Lundi* (13)	Sept. 16
Aug. 3	Sainte-Beuve, *Portraits Contemporains*	Sept. 16
Aug. 3	Greville, *Life of Sir Philip Sidney*	Aug. 26
Aug. 17	Dicey, *Six Months in the Federal States* (2)	Aug. 24
Aug. 17	Tyndall, *Heat Considered as . . . Motion*	Aug. 24
Aug. 24	Atkinson, *Recollections of Tartar Steppes*	Sept. 3

1 8 6 3		1 8 6 3
Aug. 27	Dicey, *Six Months in the Federal States* (1)	Sept. 3
Aug. 27	Russell, *My Diary North and South*	Sept. 3
Sept. 1	*Mabinogion, The* (3)	Dec. 12
Sept. 1	Weale, *Quarterly Papers on Architecture* (3)	Oct. 14
Sept. 16	Sainte-Beuve, *Causeries du Lundi* (5, 12)	Oct. 31
Sept. 21	Russell, *My Diary North and South*	Sept. 29
Oct. 1	Varnhagen von Ense, *Tagebücher* (5)	Oct. 2
Oct. 2	Sadi, *Lustgarten*	*Mar. 11
Oct. 5	Sainte-Beuve, *Portraits de Femmes*	*Jan. 27
Oct. 5	Sainte-Beuve, *Nouveaux Lundis* (1)	Oct. 14
Oct. 16	Sadi, *Gulistan* (tr. Eastwick)	*Feb. 4
Oct. 16	*Magasin Encyclopédique* (8)	Oct. 31
Oct. 16	Chardin, *Voyages en Perse* (5)	Oct. 31
Oct. 31	*Magasin Encyclopédique* (9)	Dec. 2
Oct. 31	Sainte-Beuve, *Portraits Littéraires* (1)	Dec. 2
Oct. 31	Sainte-Beuve, *Causeries du Lundi* (1)	Dec. 2
Dec. 2	Arnold, *On Translating Homer*	Dec. 8
Dec. 2	Arnold, *On Translating Homer: Last Words*	Dec. 8
Dec. 2	Sainte-Beuve, *Causeries du Lundi* (7)	*Jan. 6
Dec. 2	Sainte-Beuve, *Portraits Contemporains* (2)	Dec. 11
Dec. 11	Gilchrist, *Life of William Blake* (1, 2)	Dec. 19

1 8 6 4

Jan. 27	Arnold, *On Translating Homer*	Apr. 12
Jan. 30	Sainte-Beuve, *Causeries du Lundi* (8, 9)	Mar. 16
Feb. 10	Varnhagen von Ense, *Tagebücher* (5)	Mar. 16
Feb. 27	Gladstone, *Wedgwood; an Address*	Mar. 2
Feb. 27	Sainte-Beuve, *Nouveaux Lundis* (2)	Mar. 11
Mar. 16	Landor, *Heroic Idylls*	Mar. 19
Mar. 16	Stanhope, *Letters* (1)	Mar. 26
Mar. 16	Hervey, *Memoirs of the Reign of Geo. II.* (1)	Mar. 26
Mar. 19	Sadi, *Rosengarten*	Mar. 30
Mar. 26	Hervey, *Memoirs of the Reign of Geo. II.* (2)	Apr. 29
Mar. 26	Malcolm, *History of Persia* (1, 2)	Apr. 14
Apr. 5	*Revue des Deux Mondes* (Sept., Oct., 1863)	May 30
Apr. 5	*Juvenal, Persius, Sulpicia etc.* (Bohn)	May 9
Apr. 12	Sainte-Beuve, *Portraits Contemporains* (3)	May 30
Apr. 14	Malcolm, *History of Persia* (1)	May 9

1 8 6 4		1 8 6 4
Apr. 29	Gilchrist, *Life of William Blake* (2)	May 6
May 9	Renan, *Vie de Jésus*	May 20
May 20	Gilchrist, *Life of William Blake* (1)	May 27
July 9	Varnhagen von Ense, *Denkwürdigkeiten etc.* (6)	Aug. 18
July 12	Mohl, *Madame Récamier* (1, 2)	Sept. 2
July 14	Giddings, *History of the Rebellion*	J[uly] 20
Aug. 1	Macpherson, *Poems of Ossian, Orrann etc.*	Aug. 18
Aug. 18	Bruce, *Life of Sir Wm. Napier* (1)	Aug. 26
Aug. 19	Epinay, *Mémoires* (1)	Aug. 27
Aug. 26	Bruce, *Life of Sir William Napier* (2)	Sept. 2
Aug. 27	Epinay, *Mémoires* (2)	Oct. 17
Sept. 10	Duclos, *Mémoires Secrets* (1, 2)	Oct. 15
Sept. 10	Lieber, *Reminiscences of . . . Niebuhr*	Oct. 29
Oct. 8	*Revue des Deux Mondes* (Aug. 15, 1864)	Oct. 15
Oct. 15	Auerbach, *Gesammelte Schriften* (7, 8)	Oct. 26
Oct. 15	Chasles, *Virginie de Leyva*	Oct. 22
Oct. 24	Capefigue, *Ninon de l'Enclos*	Oct. 26
Oct. 26	Karr, *Tour Round My Garden*	Nov. 15
Nov. 15	*Macmillan's Magazine* (May, 1864)	Nov. 22
Dec. 10	Charles, *Roger Bacon: sa Vie etc.*	Dec. 17
Dec. 20	Brewster, *Memoirs of Sir Isaac Newton* (1, 2)	*Feb. 15
Dec. 20	Brightwell, *A Life of Linnæus*	Dec. 10
Dec. 17	Sainte-Beuve, *Portraits de Femmes*	Dec. 19
Dec. 17	Sainte-Beuve, *Nouveaux Lundis* (2)	Dec. 19
Dec. 17	*Cornhill Magazine* (Aug., 1864)	Dec. 22
Dec. 17	Snorri, *Heimskringla* (Laing) (3)	Dec. 19
Dec. 27	Renan, *The Life of Jesus*	*Mar. 8

1 8 6 5

Feb. 15	(Rec'd Subscription for 1865)	
Mar. 4	Randolph, *Life of General Wilson* (2)	Apr. 11
Mar. 4	Saint Simon, *Mémoires Complèts* (1)	May 13
Mar. 15	Bruce, *Life of Sir William Napier* (1)	Mar. 27
Mar. 30	Dudevant, *Simon*	Apr. 18
Apr. 11	Emerson, *Poems*	May 11
Apr. 18	*Fraser's Magazine* (70)	Apr. 24
Apr. 24	Bates, *The Naturalist on the Amazon* (1, 2)	June 6
Apr. 24	Sainte-Beuve, *Portraits Littéraires* (2)	June 8

1 8 6 5		1 8 6 5
May 4	Praed, *Poems* (1)	May 13
May 13	Michelet, *Histoire de France* (7)	June 8
June 6	Butler, *Lives of the Fathers, Martyrs . . . Saints* (10, 11, 12)	June 7
June 30	Michelet, *Histoire de France* (7)	Sept. 4
June 30	Sainte-Beuve, *Portraits Littéraires* (2)	Sept. 4
July 7	Leslie, *Life . . . of Sir Joshua Reynolds* (2)	July 13
Aug. 19	Buechner, *Force and Matter*	Sept. 18
Aug. 19	Grimm, *Life of Michael Angelo* (2)	Aug. 23
Sept. 6	Mommsen, *History of Rome* (1)	Oct. 28
Sept. 6	Roland, *La Chanson de Roland* (Génin)	Oct. 10
Sept. 18	Viollet-le-Duc, *Entretiens sur l'Architecture*	Sept. 30
Oct. 28	Mommsen, *History of Rome* (1)	*Mar. 10
Oct. 28	Knight, *Popular History of England* (2)	Nov. 22
Nov. 4	Hegel, *Lectures on Philos. of History*	*Mar. 10
Nov. 21	Confucius, *Works* (Marshman)	Nov. 29
Nov. 21	*Afternoon Lectures on Eng. Lit. and Art*	Nov. 25
Nov. 22	Knight, *Popular History of England* (2)	*Jan. 25

1 8 6 6

Jan. 13	(Rec'd Subscription for 1866)	
Jan. 18	Bunsen, *Egypt's Place in Universal History* (3, 4)	Feb. 24
Jan. 25	Knight, *Popular History of England* (4)	Apr. 7
Feb. 1	Taine, *Histoire de la Littérature Anglaise* (1)	Mar. 16
Feb. 21	About, *La Prusse en 1860*	Mar. 10
Feb. 24	Bunsen, *Egypt's Place in Universal History* (3, 4)	Mar. 10
Mar. 16	Gladstone, *Studies on Homer* (1)	Apr. 14
Mar. 31	Bowles, *Across the Continent*	Apr. 7
Apr. 4	Forster, *Sämmtliche Schriften* (9)	May 22
Apr. 4	Michelet, *Histoire de France* (10)	May 22
Apr. 14	Berry, *Extracts of Journals and Correspondence* (2)	Apr. 21
Apr. 21	Sainte-Beuve, *Causeries du Lundi* (1)	May 31
May 22	Sainte-Beuve, *Causeries du Lundi* (15)	June 2
May 22	Berry, *Extracts of Journals and Correspondence* (2)	Ret'd
July 5	Homer, *Werke*, (ed. Voss)	Aug. 17
July 5	Sainte-Beuve, *Causeries du Lundi* (1)	Sept. 15
July 23	Beethoven, *Letters* (1)	July 28
July 23	Vedas, *Rig-veda-sanhitá* (4)	July 28

1 8 6 6		1 8 6 6	
Aug. 17	White, *Poetry Lyrical etc. of the Civil War*	Aug.	23
Aug. 23	Ruskin, *Ethics of the Dust*	Aug.	30
Aug. 25	Grimm, *Life of Michael Angelo* (2)	Aug.	30
Sept. 5	Small, *Handbook of Sanskrit Literature*	Sept.	8
Sept. 8	Wilkinson, *Egyptians in the Time of the Pharaohs*	Sept.	15
Sept. 8	Field, *Pear Culture*	Nov.	7
Sept. 15	Sainte-Beuve, *Causeries du Lundi* (2)	Dec.	13
Sept. 15	Michelet, *Histoire de France* (2)	Nov.	7
Oct. 2	Swinburne, *Atlanta in Calydon*	Oct.	8
Oct. 20	Field, *Hist. of the Atlantic Telegraph*	Oct.	25
Oct. 25	Beaumont and Fletcher, *Works* (ed. Dyce) (2)	Nov.	7
Oct. 31	Meteyard, *Life of Josiah Wedgwood* (1)	Nov.	24
Oct. 31	Leslie, *Life . . . of Sir Joshua Reynolds* (? 1)	Ret'd	
[Nov.] 7	Meteyard, *Life of Josiah Wedgwood* (2)	Nov.	14
Dec. 1	Meteyard, *Life of Josiah Wedgwood* (2)	Dec.	8
Dec. 1	Herodotus, *History* (ed. Rawlinson) (1)	*Jan.	5
Dec. 13	Lytton, *The Lost Tales of Miletus*	Dec.	20
Dec. 29	Fergusson, *Illus. Handbk. of Architecture* (1)	*Feb.	5

1 8 6 7

Feb. 19	Bacon, *Essays* (ed. Whately)	Ret'd	
Feb. 19	Vigny, *Cinq-Mars*	Mar.	8
Feb. 21	Thompson, *Day Dreams of a Schoolmaster*	Apr.	2
Apr. 8	*Revue des Deux Mondes* (Sept., Oct., 1866)	June	5
Apr. 8	Palgrave, *Essays on Art*	Apr.	17
Apr. 22	*North American Review* (99)	May	2
Apr. 23	Palgrave, *Narrative of a Year's Journey* (1)	May	18
May 13	Ritter, *Comparative Geography of Palestine*	May	13
May 18	Sainte-Beuve, *Causeries du Lundi* (2)	June	3
May 29	Lessing, *Sämmtliche Schriften* (10)	June	5
June 29	Legge, *Chinese Classics* (2)	Aug.	3
June 29	*Revue des Deux Mondes* (Sept., Oct., 1866)	Sept.	19
July 27	Wheeler, *History of India* (1)	Aug.	3
Aug. 13	Dudevant, *Laura*	Aug.	30
Aug. 13	Hazlitt, *Memoirs of William Hazlitt* (1)	Aug.	17
Aug. 17	Lessing, *Sämmtliche Schriften* (10)	Sept.	3
Aug. 17	Herschel, *Familiar Lectures on Scientific Subjects*	Aug.	20
Aug. 31	Carlyle, *German Romance* (1)	Sept.	28

1 8 6 7			1 8 6 7	
Sept.	3	Herschel, *Familiar Lectures on Scientific Subjects*	Sept.	10
Oct.	11	Mueller, *Lectures on the Science of Language*		
		(2nd Ser.)	Nov.	19
Oct.	11	Saint Simon, *Mémoires Complèts* (1)	Nov.	22
Oct.	14	White, *Emanuel Swedenborg* (2)	Oct.	14
Oct.	19	Marshman, *History of India* (1)	Oct.	25
Oct.	26	Arnold, *On the Study of the Celtic Literature*	Nov.	1
Nov.	15	Hugo, *Chansons des Rues et des Bois*	*Mar.	7
Nov.	22	Saint Simon, *Mémoires Complèts* (2)	Dec.	3
Nov.	22	Stanhope, *Letters* (2 or 4)	Dec.	3
Dec.	16	Dalton, *Treatise on Human Physiology*	*Jan.	14
Dec.	16	Thiers, *Hist. du Consulat et de l'Empire* (19)	*Jan.	6

1 8 6 8

Jan.	4	(Rec'd Payment)		
Jan.	6	Corneille, *Œuvres Complètes*	Jan.	9
Jan.	14	Herbert, *Life of Edward, Lord Herbert*	Feb.	18
Jan.	16	Wilkinson, *Manners . . . of Ancient Egyptians* (1)	Feb.	20
Jan.	30	Voltaire, *Œuvres Complètes* (57)	Feb.	20
Feb.	20	Voltaire, *Œuvres Complètes* (56)	Mar.	16
Feb.	26	Southey, *Book of the Church* (1)	Mar.	25
Mar.	25	Taine, *Nouveaux Essais de Critique*	May	7
Apr.	4	Mueller, *Chips from a German Workshop* (1)	Apr.	13
Apr.	18	About, *La Grèce Contemporaine*	Apr.	18
Apr.	18	Mueller, *Chips from a German Workshop* (2)	Apr.	29
Apr.	29	Sainte-Beuve, *Nouveaux Lundis* (9)	May	7
May	7	Sainte-Beuve, *Portraits Contemporains* (3)	June	17
June	18	Kavanagh, *Adèle*	Aug.	1
June	18	Sainte-Beuve, *Portraits Contemporains* (3)	Sept.	21
July	6	Wordsworth, *Poetical Works* (4)	July	11
Aug.	1	*Revue des Deux Mondes* (July-Aug., 1867)	Nov.	2
Sept.	7	Quatremère de Quincy, *Essay on . . . Fine Arts*	Sept.	9
Sept.	9	Tyndall, *Sound: Eight Lectures*	Oct.	23
Sept.	21	Wordsworth, *Athens and Attica*	Oct.	2
Sept.	26	Vitruvius Pollio, *Architecture* (Weale's Series)	Oct.	12
Oct.	24	Craik, *A Woman's Thoughts About Women*	Nov.	20
Nov.	9	Morley, *The King and the Commons*	Nov.	17
Nov.	20	Owen, *Palæontology*	*Apr.	5

1 8 6 8			1 8 6 8	
Nov.	20	Skene, *The Four Ancient Books of Wales* (1)	Nov.	31
Nov.	21	Stahr, *Weimar und Jena*	Dec.	29
Nov.	28	*Massachusetts Quarterly Review*	Dec.	1
Dec.	5	Bright, *Speeches on Questions* (1)	Dec.	11
Dec.	12	Herbert, *Life of Edward, Lord Herbert*	*Jan.	13
Dec.	15	Garbett, *Principles of Design in Archit cture* (Weale)	*Jan.	18
Dec.	26	Skene, *The Four Ancient Books of Wales* (1)	*Jan.	5
Dec.	26	Chaucer, *Works* (add'ns by Urry)	*Jan.	16

1 8 6 9

Jan.	2	Bradford, *History of Plymouth Plantation*	Feb.	9
Jan.	8	Bunsen, *A Memoir of Baron Bunsen* (1)	Feb.	13
Jan.	9	Renan, *Essais de Moral et de Critique*	Feb.	25
Jan.	9	Roland, *La Chanson de Roland*	Feb.	9
Mar.	5	*Harper's New Monthly Magazine* (10)	Mar.	22
Mar.	8	*Parliamentary History of England* (4)	Mar.	27
Mar.	20	Wordsworth, *Poetical Works* (4)	Mar.	27
Mar.	29	Tholuck, *Blüthensämmlung*	Apr.	22
Apr.	6	Garbett, *Rudimentary Treatise*	Apr.	10
Apr.	10	Euripides, *Tragedies* (Bohn ed.) (1)	May	28
Apr.	10	Wieland, *Sämmtliche Werke* (47, 48)	May	30
Apr.	16	*Edinburgh Review* (Jan., 1869)	May	22
May	1	Wieland, *Sämmtliche Werke* (15, 16)	May	4
May	4	Wieland, *Sämmtliche Werke* (27, 28)	May	8
May	4	Heyse, *Vier neue Novellen*	May	5
May	6	Bunsen, *A Memoir of Baron Bunsen* (2)	May	8
May	8	Wieland, *Sämmtliche Werke* (5, 6)	May	11
May	11	Wieland, *Sämmtliche Werke* (21, 22)	May	26
May	22	Dwyer, *On Seats and Saddles*	June	2
July	6	Taine, *The Ideal in Art*	June	12
July	23	*Bibliotheca Classica Latina*	Aug.	30
Aug.	9	Wieland, *Sämmtliche Werke* (29, 30)	Aug.	30
Aug.	16	Thompson, *Sales Attici*	Aug.	31
Aug.	30	Schwegler, *Handbk of the Hist. of Philosophy*	Sept.	30
Sept.	2	Homer, *Batrachomyomachia etc.* (tr. Chapman, ed. Hooper)	Dec.	4
Sept.	2	Hesiodus, *Works of Hesiod* (Bohn)	Sept.	30

1 8 6 9			1 8 6 9	
Sept.	16	Layard, *Ninevah and its Remains*	Ret'd	
Oct.	2	Longman, *History of Edward III.* (1)	Oct.	8
Oct.	21	Shairp, *Studies in Poetry and Philosophy*	Oct.	27
Nov.	23	Lubbock, *Pre-historic Times*	Mar.	28
Nov.	25	Wezel, *Belphegor* (1, 2)	Dec.	4
Dec.	6	Dibdin, *Bibliomania; or, Book-madness*	Dec.	7
Dec.	7	Marsh, *Man and Nature*	Dec.	31
Dec.	24	Buchanan, *Ballad Stories*	Dec.	31
Dec.	27	Burton, *The Book Hunter*	*Jan.	6

1 8 7 0

Jan.	18	(Rec'd Subscription)		
Jan.	22	Schiller, *Correspondence between S. and Goethe*	Mar.	21
Jan.	29	Varnhagen von Ense, *Blätter* (3)	Mar.	7
Feb.	5	Lanfrey, *Histoire de Napoléon* (2)	Feb.	17
Feb.	17	Varnhagen von Ense, *Tagebücher*	Mar.	7
Mar.	3	Waring, *Hymns and Meditations*	[?June]	1
Mar.	7	Varnhagen von Ense, *Tagebücher* (10)	Apr.	23
Mar.	15	Dumont, *Recollections of Mirabeau*	Apr.	2
Apr.	25	Lewes, *Life and Works of Goethe* (2)	May	14
Apr.	25	Steffens, *Story of My Career As Student*	May	14
May	21	Ruskin, *The Queen of the Air*	May	23
June	20	Phelps, *Hedged In*	July	17
June	30	Kavanagh, *Adèle*	July	20
July	7	Varnhagen von Ense, *Tagebücher* (9)	July	27
July	11	Bergmann, *The San Grëal*	July	15
July	13	*Lyra Apostolica*	Aug.	5
July	13	Varnhagen von Ense, *Tagebücher* (8)	Sept.	1
July	15	Reade, *Cloister and the Hearth*	Sept.	18
Aug.	12	Fustel de Coulanges, *La Cité Antique*	Sept.	17
Sept.	1	Waring, *Hymns and Meditations*	*Jan.	14
Sept.	17	*Revue des Deux Mondes* (Mar., Apr., 1864)	Oct.	27
Sept.	17	Fustel de Coulanges, *La Cité Antique*	Oct.	12
Oct.	22	Huxley, *Lay Sermons, Addresses etc.*	Oct.	29
Oct.	22	*Lyra Apostolica*	Oct.	29
Oct.	22	Hufeland, *The Art of Prolonging Life* (2)	Oct.	24
Oct.	27	*Revue des Deux Mondes* (Mar.-Apr., 1866)	Nov.	3
Oct.	27	Dryden, *Works* (17)	Oct.	28

1 8 7 0			1 8 7 0	
Oct.	28	Dante, *Opere* (4)	Nov.	3
Nov.	4	Pindarus, *Carmina et Fragmenta* (2)	*Jan.	11
Nov.	10	Oliver, *The Puritan Commonwealth*	*Jan.	13
Nov.	21	Bassanville, *Les Salons d'Autrefois* (1)	Dec.	6
Nov.	28	Bassanville, *Les Salons d'Autrefois* (3)	Dec.	28
Dec.	5	Holmes, *System of Surgery* (2)	*Jan.	13
Dec.	6	Bassanville, *Les Salons d'Autrefois* (2)	Dec.	16
Dec.	28	Hardenberg, *Henry of Ofterdingen*	*Feb.	8

1 8 7 1

Jan.	4	Bassanville, *Les Salons d'Autrefois* (4)	Jan.	5
Jan.	16	Horatius, *Opera* (ed. Stallbaum)	Mar.	11
Jan.	16	Bassanville, *Les Salons d'Autrefois* (4)	Mar.	24
Jan.	31	Holmes, *System of Surgery* (1)	Mar.	22
Feb.	4	Greville, *Certaine Learned . . . Workes*	Mar.	11
Feb.	4	Greville, *Works* (ed. Grosart) (2)	Feb.	14
Apr.	8	Brace, *The New West*	June	24
Apr.	8	Hittell, *Resources of California*	June	24
Apr.	15	Blackie, *War Songs of the Germans*	Apr.	29
June	26	Taylor, *Edwin the Fair*	July	12
July	12	Murger, *Le Sabot Rouge*	Aug.	10
Aug.	10	Herbert, *Life of Edward, Lord Herbert*	Oct.	11
Sept.	15	Ruskin, *Two Paths*	Apr.	9
Oct.	11	Victoria, *Early Years of the Prince Consort*	Dec.	30
Dec.	13	Tottel, *Songs and Sonettes* (ed. Arber)	Dec.	28
Dec.	28	Varnhagen von Ense, *Tagebücher* (10)	*Jan.	27

1 8 7 2

Jan.	20	(Rec'd Subscription)		
Jan.	22	M'Crie, *Life of John Knox*	Jan.	27
Jan.	22	Victoria, *Early Years of the Prince Consort*	Apr.	1
Jan.	24	*Mabinogion, The* (2)	Apr.	27
Mar.	16	Jamieson, *Popular Ballads and Songs* (1, 2)	Apr.	[1]
Apr.	23	Skene, *The Four Ancient Books of Wales* (1)	May	25
May	6	Wordsworth, *Poetical Works* (3)	May	7
May	14	Dudevant, *Mlle. Merquem*	May	21
May	21	Patin, *Etudes sur la Poésie Latine* (1)	May	25
June	5	Patin, *Etudes sur la Poésie Latine* (1)	June	29

1 8 7 2		1 8 7 2
June 13	Mueller, *Lectures on the Science of Religion*	June 24
June 18	Frere, *Works in Verse and Prose* (2)	June 25
June 29	Skene, *The Four Ancient Books of Wales* (1)	Oct. 10
[ ] 10	Cousin, *Jacqueline Pascal*	Nov. 16
Sept. 26	Witte, *Dante-Forschungen*	*Jan. 11
Nov. 12	Ware, *Zenobia; or, The Palmyra* (1, 2)	Dec. 7
Dec. 7	Lowell, *Poetical Works* (1)	Dec. 31
Dec. 7	Haweis, *Thought for the Times: Sermons*	Dec. 21
Dec. 31	Lowell, *Poetical Works* (2)	Dec. 31
Dec. 31	Taine, *Notes sur Paris*	*Jan. 25
Dec. 31	U. S. Dept. of Agriculture, *Report . . . for . . . 1865*	*Feb. 26

1 8 7 3

| Feb. 5 | Froude, *English in Ireland* | Feb. 10 |

1 8 1 7

Oct.	17	Goldsmith, *History of England* (1)	....
Nov.	21	Shakespeare, *Works* (2)	....
Dec.	19	Shakespeare, *Works* (4)	....

1 8 1 8

Feb.	20	Hume, *History of England* (1)	....
Mar.	20	Priestley, *Lectures on History* (1)	....
Apr.	4	*Encyclopædia* (9)	....
Apr.	10	*Encyclopædia* (5)	....
May	8	*Encyclopædia* (1)	....
June	5	Priestley, *Lectures on History* (2)	....
June	12	Johnson, *Works* (*Hawkins*) (7)	....
June	19	Hume, *History of England* (2)	....
July	3	Hume, *History of England* (3)	....
July	10	Hume, *History of England* (4)	....
July	31	Hume, *History of England* (5)	....

[1 8 2 3] *

Mar.	?	Dryden, *Miscellaneous Works* (2)	....
Mar.	?	Robertson, *History of Scotland* (1)	....
Mar.	?	Sully, *Memoirs* (tr. Lennox) (1)	....

---

*There is a gap in the Harvard Library Records at this point. The bound volumes covering Emerson's Sophomore, Junior and Senior years (Sept., 1818, through the summer of 1821), as well as those immediately following, have been lost. Only "Charging Slips," moreover, appear to have been used for the years 1823 through 1825, and the three bearing Emerson's signature have been reproduced at the beginning of this volume. The first two must be dated conjecturally. My reason for assigning the first to 1823 is that Emerson wrote from Boston (*ca.* April 8, 1823—See Rusk, *Letters,* I, 130-131) mentioning Sully's *Memoirs:* "Did you ever read Sully's *Memoirs?* I suppose I might as well ask—did you ever see a whale? the book is so little read. I got deep in the volumes by accident and as I abhor the leaving of a book half-read, am forced to finish it. On some accounts & in some places it is prodigiously interesting; but the bulk is every where disproportionate to the consequence of the affairs. ... Hume, in a single page, will often give a more distinct & perfect account of an course of events, than Sully will, of the same, in a whole voluminous chapter. So much to give vent to my wrath against the Duke." (Note "volumes" and "it"). I have transferred the first listings on each of the three slips to the end, for they seem to have been added to the top because of space shortage below.

1 8 2 3

Mar.	?	South, *Sermons* (1)	. . . .
Mar.	10	Jonson, *Works* (6)	. . . .
Mar.	17	Mosheim, *An Ecclesiastical History* (1)	. . . .
Mar.	17	Barthélemy, *Travels of Anacharsis* (4)	. . . .
Apr.	27	South, *Sermons* (2, 3, 4, 5)	. . . .
Apr.	27	Butler, *Sermons*	. . . .
[?]	?	Jonson, *Works* (7)	. . . .
Aug.	4	Sullivan, *Hist. of the District of Maine*	. . . .
[?]	?	Montaigne, *Essays* (1, 2)	. . . .
[?]	?	Shakespeare, *Works* (5)	. . . .

[1 8 2 4]*

Feb.	?	Bayle, *Dictionary, Historical and Critical* (5)	. . . .
Feb.	25	Butler, *Sermons* (4) [MS. reads "Buller"]	. . . .
Feb.	25	Bayle, *Dictionary, Historical and Critical* (4)	. . . .
[?]	24	Tillotson, *Works* (3)	. . . .
[?]	24	Barrow, *Theological Works* (2)	. . . .
[?]	?	Priestley, *Letters on Religion*	. . . .
[?]	?	Dryden, *Miscellaneous Works* (1)	. . . .
[?]	?	Balguay, *Tracts*	. . . .
July	21	*Edinburgh Review* (13)	. . . .
[?]	?	Mitford, *History of Greece* (3)	. . . .

1 8 2 5

Feb.	14	*Edinburgh Review* (17)	. . . .
Feb.	14	Newton, *Chronology of Ancient Kingdoms*	. . . .
Feb.	14	Pope, *Works* (3)	. . . .
Feb.	14	Mitford, *History of Greece* (2)	. . . .
Feb.	15	Bible (*New Testament*): (ed. Joannes Clericus) (2)	. . . . . .
Feb.	15	Hammond, *Paraphrase and Annotations*	. . . .
Feb.	17	Wollaston, *Religion of Nature Delineated*	. . . .
Feb.	17	Fenelon, *Œuvres* (2)	. . . .

---

*I date this slip 1824 chiefly because the listings resemble those of 1823. There is evidence in his *Letters* (q.v.) that he read theological works during both years. It is possible, however, that this slip is a continuation of that for 1825. If they are combined, we might well understand how such a reading program could lead to Emerson's physical breakdown and serious eye trouble in March, 1825, after but three months at the Divinity School (January-March). Combined they suggest that he eagerly desired to take advantage of his opportunities at Harvard.

1 8 2 5   1 8 2 5

Feb.	17	Leibnitz, *Essais de Théodicée*	. . . .
Feb.	20	*Boyle Lecture Sermons* (ed. Lettsome) (2)	. . . .
Feb.	20	Hume, *Essays and Treatises* (2)	. . . .
Feb.	20	Hume, *History of England* (3, 4, 5)	. . . .

1 8 2 6 *

Mar.	30	Mitford, *History of Greece* (1)	(C. C. Emerson)
Mar.	30	Middleton, *Life of Cicero* (1)	(C. C. Emerson)
[?]	?	Mitford, *History of Greece* (4)	. . . .
[?]	?	Montaigne, *Essays* (1)	. . . .
Mar.	31*	. . . .	. . . .
Apr.	13	Montaigne, *Essays* (1)	(C. C. Emerson)
Apr.	24	Jonson, *Works* (1)	(W. Emerson)
June	12	Bacon, *Works* (Mallet) (2)	(W. Emerson)
Aug.	7	Burke, *Works* (5)	(W. Emerson)
Aug.	7	Montaigne, *Essays* (3)	(W. Emerson)
Sept.	4	Davila, *Hist. of the Civil Wars of France* (1)	. . . .
Sept.	4	Bacon, *Works* (Mallet) (7)	. . . .
Oct.	9*	. . . .	. . . .
Nov.	2	Plato, *Works of Plato* (4)	. . . .
Nov.	2	Plutarch, *Œuvres* (Amyot) (15)	. . . .
Nov.	16	Plutarch, *Œuvres* (Amyot) (15)	. . . .
Nov.	16	Stewart, *Philos. of the Human Mind* (2)	. . . .
Nov.	16	Antoninus, *Meditations* (Collier)	. . . .
Nov.	16	Coleridge, *Biographia Literaria*	. . . .

1 8 2 7

July	30	Montaigne, *Essays* (2)	. . . .
Dec.	3	Plato, *Works of Plato* (4)	. . . .
Dec.	3	Plutarch, *Œuvres* (Amyot) (4)	. . . .

---

*The records make it clear that Charles and William withdrew the books indicated below for Waldo's use. The Emerson family and their friends often withdrew and returned books vicariously, as the Charging Records both of Harvard Library and of the Boston Athenæum indicate. (On Oct. 9, 1826, Waldo withdrew a book for William, and signed for it under William's name.) The Harvard records do not, as a rule, indicate the date on which books were returned. The charge was merely crossed off. On the last leaf of the record of loans to Officers and Graduates of the college for 1825-1826, however, Waldo is listed as having returned to the library, on March 31, [1826?], Montaigne's *Essays* (vol. 2) and Voltaire's *State of Europe* (vol. 1).

1 8 2 8

Jan.	14	Enfield, *History of Philosophy* (1)	....
Mar.	21	Beloe, *History of Herodotus* (2)	....
Mar.	21	Johnson, *Works* (Hawkins) (14)	....
Mar.	24	Locke, [*Familiar Letters*]	....
Apr.	11	Burke, *Works* (5)	....
June	12	Saint-Evremond, *Works* (1, 2)	....
July	23	Hobbes, [*Works*] (1, 2)	....
July	23	Saint-Evremond, *Works* (? 3)	....
July	23	Wotton, [*Reliquiæ Wottonianæ*]	....
July	28	Smith, *Introd. to Physiological . . . Botany*	....
July	28	Cooper, *Characteristics of Men* (1, 2)	....
Aug.	1	Bigelow, *Florula Bostoniensis*	....
Aug.	12	Sarpi, *Historie of the Councel of Trent*	....
Sept.	1	Plutarch, *Œuvres* (Amyot) (14, 19)	....
Sept.	22	Davy, *Elements of Chemical Philosophy*	....
Nov.	24	Jonson, *Works* (6)	....
Nov.	24	Volney, *The Ruins*	....
Dec.	5	Goethe, *Werke* (Stuttgart) (3)	....

1 8 2 9

Feb.	1	Herder, *Outlines Phil. of Hist. of Man* (ed. 1800)	....
Feb.	1	Antoninus, *Meditations* (Collier)	....
Feb.	16	Chalmers, *Works of the English Poets* (3)	....
Feb.	16	Porson, *Letters to Archdeacon Travis*	....
Feb.	16	Hutchinson, *History of Massachusetts* (3)	....
Apr.	22	Plato, *Works of Plato* (4)	....

1 8 3 1

Jan.	21	United States: *State Papers* (1801-1806)	(C. C. Emerson)
Jan.	21	Hamilton, *Works* (1)	(C. C. Emerson)
Feb.	28	Marsh, *Introduction to New Testament* (1)	(C. C. Emerson)

1 8 3 2

Sept.	18	North, *Examen; or An Enquiry*	....

1 8 3 4

Dec.	10	Vasari, *Vite de' Piu Excellenti Pittori* (8, 14)	....
Dec.	10	Buonarrot [prob. Michael Angelo]	....

,1 8 3 5 *

July	20	Spenser, *Poetical Works* (Upton) (7-8)	. . . .
July	20	Sidney, *Miscellaneous Works*	. . . .
July	20	Shakespeare, *Plays and Poems* (Malone) (1)	. . . .
July	20	Massachusetts Historical Soc., *Collections* (II.5)	. . . .
July	20	Hooker, *Lawes of Ecclesiastical Politie*	. . . .

1 8 4 6

Sept.	2	Hone, *Ancient Mysteries Described*	. . . .
Sept.	2	Plato, *Platons Werke* (Schleiermacher) (1)	. . . .
Sept.	2	Chodzko, *Specimens of Poetry of Persia*	. . . .
Sept.	2	Firdausi, *The Sháh Námeh* (Atkinson)	. . . .
Nov.	18	Upham, *Hist. and Doctrine of Budhism*	. . . .
Nov.	18	Sadi, *The Gulistan* (tr. Ross)	. . . .
Nov.	18	*Ana, ou Collection des Bons Mots* (10)	. . . .
Nov.	18	Callaway (tr.), *Yakkun Nattanawā*	. . . .
Nov.	18	Pelet, *Napoleon in Council*	. . . .

1 8 4 7

Jan.	14	Jamieson, *Popular Ballads and Songs* (1, 2)	. . . .
Jan.	14	*Ancient Scottish Poems*	. . . .
Jan.	14	*Lays of the Minnesingers*	. . . .
Jan.	14	*English Poets* (17)	. . . .
Mar.	30	Ward, *Acc't of the Writings of the Hindoos* (1)	. . . .
Mar.	30	Ozanam, *Dante et la Philosophie Catholique*	. . . .
Mar.	30	Boeckh, *Public Economy of Athens*	. . . .
July	26	Chodzko, *Specimens of Poetry of Persia*	. . . .
July	26	Firdausi, *The Sháh Námeh* (Atkinson)	. . . .
July	26	Mallet, *Northern Antiquities* (Bohn)	. . . .
July	26	Charlevoix, *Journal of Voyage to N. America* (1, 2)	. . . .

1 8 4 8

Nov.	8	Greville, *Certaine Learned and Elegant Workes*	. . . .
Nov.	8	Schleiermacher, *Introd. to Dialogues of Plato*	. . . .
Nov.	8	Ast, *Platon's Leben und Schriften*	. . . .
Nov.	8	Lowth, *Life of William of Wykeham*	. . . .

*These books were carried forward in the new loan record begun in September.

1 8 4 8   1 8 4 8

Nov. 8   Collins, *Peerage of England* (1)   . . . .

Nov. 8   Sewell, *An Introd. to Dialogues of Plato*   . . . .

1 8 4 9

Mar. 14 Hooker, *Genera Filicum*   . . . .

Mar. 14 Goethe, *Œuvres d'Histoire Naturelle*   . . . .

1 8 5 0

Apr. 16 Voltaire [*Œuvres*] (20, 21)   July   1

1 8 5 5

May 18   *Mabinogion, The* (1, 2)   . . . .

May 18   Vasari, *Vite de' Piu Excellenti Pittori* (14)   . . . .

May 18   Niebuhr, *Lectures on Ancient Ethnography* (1)   . . . .

May 18   Niebuhr, *Lectures on History of Rome* (1)   . . . .

May 18   Niebuhr, *Life and Letters* (3)   . . . .

1 8 6 8

Feb. 20 Sewell, *An Introd. to Dialogues of Plato*   . . . .

Mar. 25 Preller, ⎧ [? *Die Regionem der Stadt Rom*]   . . . .
                    ⎨ [? *Römische Mythologie*]
                    ⎩ [? *Ausgewählte Aufsätze*]

HARVARD DIVINITY SCHOOL*

1 8 2 7

Nov.	30	Hales, *Golden Remains*	. . . .
Nov.	30	Taylor, *Whole Works* (2, 11)	. . . .
Dec.	15	Taylor, *Whole Works* (11)	. . . .
Dec.	18	Taylor, *Whole Works* (8)	. . . .

1 8 2 8

. . . . . .		Taylor, *Whole Works* (3, 6, 11)	. . . .
Jan.	16	Warburton, *Works* (12)	. . . .
Jan.	16	Belsham, *The Epistles of Paul the Apostle* (1)	([M. I.] Motte)
Jan.	16	Butler, *Reminiscences of Charles Butler*	([M. I.] Motte)
June	25	Taylor, *Whole Works* (5)	. . . .
July	9	*Quarterly Review* (35)	. . . .
July	9	Milton, *[Poetical] Works* (1)	. . . .
July	18	Taylor, *Whole Works* (2, 3, 5)	. . . .
July	24	Butler, *Reminiscences of Charles Butler*	. . . .
Sept.	6	Wordsworth, *[Poetical Works]* (3, 4)	. . . .
Nov.	8	Blackstone, *[Commentaries on the Laws of England]* (1, 2)	. . . .

1 8 2 9

. . . . . .		Wordsworth, *[Poetical Works]* (4)	. . . .
Feb.	4	Milton, *[Selection from English] Prose Works* (2)	. . . .
. . . . . .		Taylor, *Whole Works* (5, 6)	. . . .
. . . . . .		Lardner, *Works* (Life by Kippis) (3)	. . . .

---

* The library of the Harvard Divinity School in Cambridge, Mass., is known as the "Andover-Harvard Theological Library," a result of the combining of bibliographical resources of two schools. See "List of Books Taken Out, 1826-1842," a MS. volume bearing the call number: 400.27. Emerson borrowings appear on folio 113. Emerson signed for all the volumes except the two removed for him by a classmate.

EMERSON BIBLIOGRAPHY

1) The numbers to the left of each item are those used in the index at the end of this bibliography.

2) The symbols to the right of the "item numbers" refer to the foregoing lists of reading. For example, "H18" means Harvard College Library, 1818"; "B70" means "Boston Athenæum Library, 1870"; "HD28" means "Harvard Divinity School Library, 1828." See the earlier pages for volume numbers used in the years indicated.

3) When two or more editions (or titles) are given under a number, the compiler is uncertain which was used. An asterisk (*) indicates reasonable certainty.

A

(1)   B68
ABOUT, Edmond François Valentin
    La Grèce Contemporaine
        Paris, 1854

(2)   B57
ABOUT, Edmond François Valentin
    Greece and the Greeks of the Present Day
        New York and London, 1857

(3)   B66
ABOUT, Edmond François Valentin
    La Prusse en 1860
        Paris, 1860

(4)   B32
ACOSTA, Joseph de
    Naturall and Morall Histoire of the East and West Indies
        London, 1604   (2 copies. Emerson used copy 1)

(5)   B61
ADAMS, John Quincy *Pres. of the U. S.*
    Lectures on Rhetoric and Oratory
        Cambridge (Mass.), 1810   (2 vols.)

(6)   B37
ÆSCHYLUS
    Tragedies (tr. by Robert Potter)
        London, 1819

(7)   B65
AFTERNOON LECTURES
    The Afternoon Lectures on English Literature and Art, delivered
    in Dublin   [First]—Fifth Series
        London, 1863-1869   (5 vols.)

(8)   B62
ALISON, *Sir* Archibald, *bart.*
    Lives of Lord Castlereagh and Sir Charles Stewart, the Second
    and Third Marquesses of Londonderry
        Edinburgh, 1861   (3 vols.)

(9)   H46
ANA
    Ana, ou Collection de Bons Mots, Contes, . . . Anecdotes des
    Hommes Célèbres [comp. by Charles G. T. Garnier]
        Amsterdam, [1799]   (10 vols.)

(10)   B62
ANCIENT COSTUME   (vol. 3)
    (Thomas Hope's *Costume of the Ancients* has only two volumes.
    It is possible that the "3" was an error for "1" and that the
    reference is to Hope's work. The loan record gives the shelf
    number "F21" to both. Other possibilities are:
        Bardon, M. F. D.
            Costume des Anciens
               Paris, 1784-1786   (4 parts)   (Nouv. éd.)
        Malliot, J.
            Costumes . . . des anciens peuples
               Paris, 1809   (3 vols.)

(11) H47

ANCIENT SCOTTISH POEMS
Ancient Scottish Poems, published from the MS. of George
Bannatyne, 1568, (ed. Sir David Dalrymple, Lord Hailes)
Edinburgh, 1770
London, 1815 (reprint)

(12) B57

ANDERSEN, Hans Christian
Danish Fairy Legends and Tales
London, 1846

(13) B31

ANDERSON, Robert *M.D., editor*
Works of the British Poets
London, 1795-1815 (14 vols.)
Vol. 3: Drayton, Carew, Suckling

(14) B32, B36

ANNUAL
Annual Register: or, View of the History, Politics, and Litera-
ture
London (Dodsley), 1762-1867 (103 vols.)

(15) B45

ANTOMMARCHI, Francesco
The Last Days of the Emperor Napoleon
London, 1825 (2 vols.)

(16) H26, H29

ANTONINUS, Marcus Aurelius *Imperator Romæ*
[Meditations, i.e.,] Conversation with Himself. With prelim. dis-
course of Gataker. Also the Emperor's Life by M. D'Acier.
Added: the mythological picture of Cebes. Tr. into English by
Jeremy Collier
London, 1708 (2nd ed. corrected)

(17) B57

ARAGO, Dominique François Jean
Biographies of Distinguished Scientific Men. (tr. by W. H. Smyth,
Baden Powell, and Robert Grant)
London, 1857

(18) B61

ARGENSON, René Louis de Voyer, *marquis de*
Journal et Mémoires (pub. par E. J. B. Rathery)
Paris (Société de l'Histoire de France), 1859-1864 (7 vols.)

(19) B37

ARIOSTO, Lodovico
The Orlando Furioso (tr. into English verse by Wm. Stewart Rose)
*London, 1823-1831 (8 vols.)

(20) B36

ARISTOPHANES
Comedies of Aristophanes (tr. Thomas Mitchell)
London, 1820-1822 (2 vols.)
Vol. 1: "Preliminary Discourse on Aristophanes"

(21) B30

ARISTOPHANES
Comœdiæ ex optimis exemplaribus emendatæ: cum versione latina,
variis lectionibus, notis, et emendationibus . . . A Rich. Franc.
Phil. Brunck
Oxford, 1810 (4 vols.)

(22)   B36
ARISTOTLE
    Aristotle's Ethics and Politics   (tr. John Gillies)
            London, 1813   (3rd ed., 2 vols.)
                    Vol. 2: "Politics"

(23)   B62
ARNOLD, Matthew
    Merope. A Tragedy
            London, 1858

(24)   B67
ARNOLD, Matthew
    On the Study of Celtic Literature
            London, 1867

(25)   B62, B63, B64
ARNOLD, Matthew
    On Translating Homer. Three Lectures given at Oxford
            London, 1861

(26)   B63
ARNOLD, Matthew
    On Translating Homer: Last Words
            London, 1862

(27)   H48
AST, Friedrich
    Platon's Leben und Schriften
            Leipzig, 1816

(28)   B63
ATKINSON, [Lucy)] (*Mrs*. Thomas Witlam)
    Recollections of Tartar Steppes and their Inhabitants
            London, 1863

(29)   B37
AUDUBON, John James
    Ornithological Biography: or, an account of the habits of birds
        of the U. S., with descriptions of objects in [his] "The Birds
        of America"
            Edinburgh, 1831-1849 (i.e., 1839)   (5 vols.)
            Philadelphia, 1831-1839   (5 vols.)

(30)   B64
AUERBACH, Berthold
    Gesammelte Schriften
            Stuttgart und Augsburg, 1857-1858   (20 bde.)
                    Vol. 7: "Der Lehnhold"; Vol. 8: "Ein eigen Haus"

(31)   B61
AUSTEN, Jane
    Pride and Prejudice
            London, 1817   (2 vols.)
            London, 1853   (2 vols.)

(32)   B34, B35, B37
AUSTIN, *Mrs*. Sarah (Taylor)
    Characteristics of Goethe: from the German of Falk, von Müller,
        etc.
            London, 1833   (3 vols.)

(33)   B36
AVESTA (*French*)
    Zend-Avesta, ouvrage de Zoroastre (tr. par Anquetil du Perron)
            Paris, 1771   (2 vols. in 3)

B

(34)   B67
BACON, Francis *Baron Verulam and Viscount St. Albans*
  Bacon's Essays (Annotations by Richard Whately)
    London, 1856

(35)   H26
BACON, Francis *Baron Verulam and Viscount St. Albans*
  Works (with his life by Mallet)
    London, 1807   (12 vols.)

(36)   B57
BACON, Francis *Baron Verulam and Viscount St. Albans*
  Works (ed. by James Spedding, R. L. Ellis, and D. D. Heath)
    London, 1857, 1856.   (7 vols.)

(37)   B32
BAILLIE, Joanna
  A Series of Plays (delineating the stronger passions of the mind)
    London, 1799-1812   (2nd ed., 3 vols.)

(38)   H24
BALGUY, John
  [Tracts]
    In 1824, some of Balguy's many pamphlets were appar-
    ently bound together and given the title "Tracts." An old
    shelf list indicates that the following were included in
    "Tracts 30":
      Law of Truth (1733)
      Letters to a Deist (1730)
      Second Letter to a Deist (1831)
      Natural Religion

(39)   B58
BANDELLO, Matteo
  Novelle di Bandello
    Milano, 1813-1814   (9 vols.)

(40)   B57
BARBIERI, Giovanni Francesco, *detto* il Guercino
  *Etchings from Guercino (by Francesco Bartolozzi)
    [London, 1764]

(41)   B35
BARCLAY, Robert
  An Apology for the True Christian Divinity, as the same is held
  forth, and preached, by the people, called in scorn, Quakers
    [t.p. of Athenæum copy missing; ed. not known.]

(42)   H24
BARROW, Isaac
  Theological Works (ed. Tillotson)
    London, 1716   (3 vols. in 2)

(43)   H23
BARTHELEMY, Jean Jacques *l'abbe*
  Travels of Anacharsis the Younger in Greece
  (A tr. of *Le Voyage de jeune Anacharsis en Grèce*)
    Philadelphia, 1804   (4 vols.)

(44)   B36
BARTRAM, William
  Travels through North and South Carolina, Florida, the Cherokee
  Country . . . with observations on the Indians
    *Philadelphia, 1791
    Dublin, 1793

(45)　　　　　　　　　　　　　　　　　　　　　　　　B70, B71
BASSANVILLE, Anais (Lebrun) *comtesse de*
　　　Les Salons d'Autrefois: souvenirs intimes
　　　　　　Paris, [1862-1866]　(3° éd., 4 tomes)

(46)　　　　　　　　　　　　　　　　　　　　　　　　　　　B65
BATES, Henry Walter
　　　The Naturalist on the River Amazons . . . Brazilian and Indian
　　　　　Life
　　　　　　London, 1863　(2 vols.)

(47)　　　　　　　　　　　　　　　　　　　　　　　　　　　B45
BAUSSET, Louis François Joseph *baron de*
　　　Private Memoirs of the Court of Napoleon (1805-1814)
　　　　　　Philadelphia, 1828

(48)　　　　　　　　　　　　　　　　　　　　　　　　　　　B30
BAXTER, Richard
　　　A Treatise of Knowledge and Love Compared
　　　　　　London, 1689

(49)　　　　　　　　　　　　　　　　　　　　　　　　　　　H24
BAYLE, Pierre
　　　The Dictionary Historical and Critical of Mr. Peter Bayle
　　　　　(With life of the author by Mr. Des Maizeaux)
　　　　　　London, 1734-1738　(5 vols.)

(50)　　　　　　　　　　　　　　　　　　　　　　　　　　　B54
BEATTIE, William *editor*
　　　Life and Letters of Thomas Campbell
　　　　　　London, 1849　(3 vols.)

(51)　　　　　　　　　　　　　　　　　　　　　　　　　　　B42
BEAUMONT, Francis; *and* John Fletcher
　　　Dramatick Works with Notes
　　　　　　*London, 1778　(10 vols.)

(52)　　　　　　　　　　　　　　　　　　　　　　　　　　　B66
BEAUMONT, Francis; *and* John Fletcher
　　　The Works of Beaumont and Fletcher (with notes and memoir by
　　　　　Alexander Dyce)
　　　　　　London, 1843-1846　(11 vols.)

(53)　　　　　　　　　　　　　　　　　　　　　　　　　　　B45
BECKFORD, William
　　　Italy, with sketches of Spain and Portugal
　　　　　　London, 1834　(2 vols.)

(54)　　　　　　　　　　　　　　　　　　　　　　　　　　　B30
BEECHEY, Frederick William; *and* H. W. Beechey
　　　Proceedings of the Expedition to explore the Northern Coast of
　　　　　Africa
　　　　　　London, 1828

(55)　　　　　　　　　　　　　　　　　　　　　　　　　　　B66
BEETHOVEN, Ludwig van
　　　Beethoven's Letters (1790-1826) from the collection of Dr. Lud-
　　　　wig Nohl; also his letters to the Archduke Rudolph from the
　　　　coll. of Dr. Ludwig ritter von Köchel. (Tr. Lady Wallace)
　　　　　　London, 1866　(2 vols.)

(56)　　　　　　　　　　　　　　　　　　　　　　　　　　　B36
BELL, *Sir* Charles
　　　Essays on the Anatomy of Expression in Painting
　　　　　　London, 1806

(57)   B52
BELL, John (1745-1831) *of London*
    Bell's British Theatre (plays with short notices)
        London, 1797   [1791-1797]   (34 vols.)

(58)   B34
BELL, John (1763-1820)
    Observations on Italy
        Edinburgh, 1825
        Boston, 1826

(59)   H28
BELOE, William *translator*
    The History of Herodotus (tr. from the Greek with notes)
        London, 1791   (4 vols.)

(60)   HD28
BELSHAM, Thomas
    The Epistles of Paul the Apostle (tr. with an exposition and notes)
        London, 1822   (4 vols.)
        London, 1822   (2 vols.)

(61)   B38
BELZONI, Giovanni Battista
    Narrative of the Operations and Recent Discoveries within the
    pyramids, temples, tombs, and excavations, in Egypt and Nubia
        London, 1822   (3rd. ed., 2 vols.)

(62)   B70
BERGMANN, Frédéric Guillaume
    The San Grëal, an inquiry into the origin and signification of the
    romances of the San Grëal
        Edinburgh, 1870

(63)   B66
BERRY, *Miss* Mary
    Extracts of the Journals and Correspondence (1783-1852), ed. by
    Lady Theresa Lewis
        London, 1865   (3 vols.)

(64)   B40
BEYLE, Marie Henri (*pseud.*, de Stendhal)
    The Lives of Haydn and Mozart, with observations on [Pietro]
    Metastasio and Present State of Music in France and Italy.
    (tr. from French of L. A. C. Bombet, *pseud.*)
        London, 1818

(65)   B32, B36
BIBER, Edward
    Henry Pestalozzi and his Plan of Education
        London, 1831

(66)   H25
BIBLE, *New Testament* (Latin) 1714. Vulgate
    Novum Testamentum Domini Nostri Jesu Christi, ex versione
    vulgata, cum paraphrasi et adnotationibus Henrici Hammondi.
    Ex anglica lingua in latinam transtulit, suisque animadver-
    sionibus illustravit, castigavit, auxit Joannes Clericus.
        Francofurti, 1714   (2nd ed., 2 vols.)

    (The entry in the Charging List—see facsimile frontispiece—
    reads "Le Clerc on N. Test." The above is the only work by
    him in the Harvard Catalogue of 1830. It is possible that the
    following work, in one of its several English editions, might
    have been used instead:

Le Clerc, Jean (1657-1736)
A Supplement to Dr. Hammond's Paraphrase and Annotations on the New Testament. . . . Likewise his Paraphrase, with notes, on the beginning of St. John's Gospel.
London, 1699.

(67)   B31

BIBLE, *New Testament* (Epistles) *English*
A New Literal Translation of all the Apostolical Epistles; with commentary, notes and life of Paul by James Macknight
Edinburgh, 1795   (2nd ed., 3 vols.)

(68)   B31

BIBLE, *N. T.* (Harmonies) *English*
Harmony of the Gospels, ed. by James Macknight
London, 1763   (2nd ed., 2 vols.)

(69)   B69

BIBLIOTHECA
Bibliotheca Classica Latina (coll. and ed. by N. E. Lemaire)
Parisiis, 1819-1833   (146 vols.)
(No volume number is given in the Loan Record. The call number, "8.21" does appear, however, and it definitely applied only to the following works, according to the available shelf-list. Emerson's choice fell within this group:
Cæsar, C. J., *Opera*   (4 vols.) 1819-1822.
Catullus, Q. V., *Opera*   (1 vol.) 1826.
Cicero, M. T.: *Orations*   (6 vols.)
Philosophia   (6 vols.)
Epistola   (3 vols.)   1821-1832

(70)   B61

BIBLIOTHECA
Bibliotheca Indica (Pub. by the Asiatic Society of Bengal)
Calcutta, 1853-1862   (3 vols. in Athenæum)

(71)   B30

BIGELOW, Jacob
American Medical Botany
Boston, 1817-1820   (3 vols.)

(72)   H28, B30

BIGELOW, Jacob
Florula Bostoniensis: A collection of plants of Boston and its environs with . . . places of growth and time of flowering and occasional remarks
Boston, 1814   (1st ed.)

(73)   B34

BIOGRAPHIE
Biographie Universelle Ancienne et Moderne
Paris, 1811-1853   (83 vols.)

(74)   B71

BLACKIE, John Stuart
War Songs of the Germans, with historical illustrations of the Liberation War and the Rhine boundary question
Edinburgh, 1870

(75)   HD28

BLACKSTONE, *Sir* William
    Commentaries on the Laws of England
        Oxford, 1768   (4 vols.)
        Portland (Mass.), 1805-1807   (4 vols.)
        Portland (Mass.), 1807   (4 vols.)   (Notes by Edward
        Christian)

(76)   B60

BLACKWOOD, Frederick Temple, *1st Marquess of Dufferin and Ava*
    A Yacht Voyage: Letters from high Latitudes; being some ac-
    count of a voyage in the schooner yacht "Foam," 850 M. to Ice-
    land, Jan Mayen, & Spitzbergen, in 1856.
        London, 1857   [Pub. in Boston in 1859.]

(77)   B32, B45, B55

BLACKWOOD'S
    Blackwood's Edinburgh Magazine
        Edinburgh, 1817-1861   (112 vols.)

(78)   B58

BLANC, Jean Joseph Louis
    1848: Historical Revelations: Inscribed to Lord Normanby
        London, 1858

(79)   H47

BOECKH (Böckh), August
    The Public Economy of Athens, with a dissertation on the silver
    mines of Laurion
        London, 1828   (2 vols.)

(80)   B62

BOISLECOMTE, André Olivier Ernest Sain
    De la Crise américaine et de celle des nationalités en Europe
        Paris, 1862

(81)   B61

BONER, Charles
    Chamois Hunting in the Mountains of Bavaria and in the Tyrol
    (Illustrated by Theodore Horschelt)
        London, 1860   (new ed.)

(82)   B62

BOOK
    The Book of Costume or, Annals of fashion, by a lady of rank
        London, 1847   (new ed.)

(83)   B63

BORROW, George
    Wild Wales: its people, language, and scenery
        London, 1862   (3 vols.)

(84)   B34, B35

BOWER, Alexander
    The Life of Luther, with an account of the early progress of the
    Reformation
        London, 1813

(85)   B66

BOWLES, Samuel
    Across the Continent: a journey to the Rocky Mountains, the
    Mormons, and the Pacific States (with Speaker Colfax)
        Springfield (Mass.), 1865

(86)   H25
[BOYLE LECTURE SERMONS]
    A Defence of Natural and Revealed Religion, being a collection
    of the sermons preached at the lecture founded by Robert
    Boyle (ed. S. Lettsome and Nicholl)
        London, 1739   (3 vols.)

(87)   B71
BRACE, Charles Loring
    The New West: or, California in 1867-1868
        New York, 1869

(88)   B61, B69
BRADFORD, William (1588-1657) *governor*
    History of Plymouth Plantation (ed. Charles Deane)
        Boston, 1856
    (This forms the greater part of vol. 33 of Mass. Hist. Soc. Coll.)

(89)   B55, B64
BREWSTER, *Sir* David
    Memoirs of the Life, Writings, and Discoveries of Sir Isaac
    Newton
        Edinburgh, 1855   (2 vols.)

(90)   B68
BRIGHT, John
    Speeches on Questions of Public Policy (ed. James E. Thorold
    Rogers)
        London, 1868   (2 vols.)

(91)   B64
BRIGHTWELL, Cecilia Lucy
    A Life of Linnæus
        London, 1858

(92)   B52
BRISTED, Charles Astor
    Five Years in an English University
        New York, 1852   (2 vols.)

(93)   B35
BRITISH ASSOCIATION for the Advancement of Science
    Report of the First [—39th] Meeting (1831-1869)
        London, 1833-1870   (38 vols.)

(94)   B51
BRITTON, John
    The History and Antiquities of the See and Cathedral Church
    of Winchester
        London, 1817

(95)   B61
BRODERIP, *Mrs.* Frances Freeling (Hood)
    Memorials of Thomas Hood, collected by his daughter, with
    preface and notes by his son [T. Hood]
        Boston, 1860   (2 vols.)

(96)   B52
BROUGHAM AND VAUX, Henry Brougham, *1st Baron*
    Speeches upon Questions relating to Public Rights, etc., and a
    diss. upon ancient eloquence
        Edinburgh, 1838   (4 vols.)

(97) B61
BROWN, Samuel (1817-1856)
    Lectures on the Atomic Theory, and Essays scientific and literary
        Edinburgh, 1858   (2 vols.)

(98) B31
BROWNE, *Sir* Thomas
    Religio Medici
        *London, 1682   (8th ed. with annotations by Sir Kenelm
        Digby.)

(99) B30
BROWNE, *Sir* Thomas
    [Tracts:] Certain Miscellany Tracts
        Edinburgh, 1822   (new ed.)

(100) B64, B65
BRUCE, Henry Austin *editor*
    Life of General Sir William Napier
        London, 1864   (2 vols.)

(101) B40
BRYANT, Jacob
    A New System, or, An Analysis of Ancient Mythology
        London, 1774-1776   (3 vols.)
        London, 1807   (3rd ed., 6 vols.)

(102) B32
BRYANT, Jacob
    The Sentiments of Philo Judæus concerning the Logos
        Cambridge (Eng.), 1797

(103) B69
BUCHANAN, Robert Williams *translator*
    Ballad Stories of the Affections (from the Scandinavian)
        London, [1869]

(104) B65
BUECHNER, Friedrich Karl Christian Ludwig
    Force and Matter (ed. and tr. from *Kraft und Stoff* by J.
    Frederick Collingwood)
        London, 1864

(105) B35
BULKLEY [Bulkeley], Peter
    The Gospel-Covenant: or The Covenant of Grace Opened
        London, 1651

(106) B66
BUNSEN, Christian Carl Josias, *freiherr* von
    Egypt's Place in Universal History (tr. Charles H. Cottrell)
        London, 1848-1867   (5 vols.)

(107) B69
BUNSEN, Frances (Waddington) *baroness*
    A Memoir of Baron Bunsen . . . drawn chiefly from family papers
    by his widow
        London, 1868   (2 vols.)

(108) H34
BUONARROTI, Michael Angelo
    (The particular volume used I cannot identify. Its classification
    is "A.3.4")

(109)   H26, H28
BURKE, Edmund
    Works
        *Boston [and New York], 1806-1813 (6 vols.) (1st
            American ed.) Vol. 5: "Miscellaneous Works" (con-
            tains speeches on America)

(110)   B40
BURNET, Gilbert *bishop of Salisbury*
    Bishop Burnet's History of His Own Time (with the author's
    life and with notes by T. Burnet)
        London, 1809   (4 vols.)

(111)   B35
BURNETT, George *editor*
    Specimens of English Prose Writers
        London, 1807   (3 vols.)

(112)   B69
BURTON, John Hill
    The Book-Hunter etc.
        Edinburgh and London, 1862

(113)   B65
BUTLER, Alban
    The Lives of the Fathers, Martyrs, and other Principal Saints
        New York, 1846   (12 vols. in 4)

(114)   HD28
BUTLER, Charles
    Reminiscences of Charles Butler
        London, 1824   (4th ed.)

(115)   H23, H24
BUTLER, [? Joseph *bishop of Durham*]
    [Sermons difficult to identify with particularity. There are *Ser-
    mons* also by Lilly Butler listed in the Harvard Catalogue of
    1830. Bishop Butler's *Works*, usually issued in two volumes,
    included (vol. 1) the *Analogy of Religion* and (vol. 2) *Fifteen
    Sermons*. Emerson might have used the *Sermons*, London,
    1749.]

C

(116)   B57
CABALA
    Cabala, sive Scrinia Sacra: mysteries of state and government
    in the reigns of Henry VIII [through Charles I]
        London, 1654

(117)   H46
CALLAWAY, John *translator*
    Yakkun Nattanawā: a Cingalese poem, descriptive of the Ceylon
    system of demonology
        London, 1829   (Oriental Translation Fund Publ. No. 7)
(118)   B52
CAMDEN, William
    Britain, or A chorographicall description of the most flourishing
    Kingdomes, England, Scotland and Ireland (tr. from Latin by
    Philemon Holland)
        *London, 1637

(119)   B51
CAMPBELL, John Campbell *1st Baron*
 The Lives of the Chief Justices of England
   London, 1849-1857 (3 vols.)

(120)   B32
CAMPBELL, Thomas
 Specimens of the British Poets
   London, 1819 (7 vols.)
     Vol. 1: "Essay on Eng. Poetry"; vol. 2: "Chaucer
      to Beaumont"

(121)   B34, B36
CANDOLLE, Alphonse; *and* Kurt Sprengel
 Elements of the Philosophy of Plants (tr. from the German)
   Edinburgh, 1821

(122)   B64
CAPEFIGUE, Jean Baptiste Honoré Raymond
 Ninon de Lenclos et les précieuses de la Place Royale
   Paris, 1864

(123)   B32
CAPPE, Newcome
 Critical Remarks on Many Important Passages of Scripture;
  together with dissertations upon several subjects (with mem-
  oirs of his life by the editor, Catherine Cappe)
   York, 1802 (2 vols.)

(124)   B58
CAREY, Henry Charles
 The Past, the Present and the Future
   Philadelphia, 1848

(125)   B58
CAREY, Henry Charles
 Principles of Social Science
   Philadelphia, 1858 (3 vols.)

(126)   B67
CARLYLE, Thomas *translator*
 German Romance: Specimens of its chief authors, with biographi-
  cal and critical notices
   Edinburgh, 1827 (4 vols.)

(127)   B45
CAULINCOURT (Caulaincourt), Armand Augustin Louis, *duc de*
 Vicence
 Recollections of Caulincourt, duke of Vicenza
   London, 1838 (2 vols.)

(128)   B31
CAVE, William
 Apostolici: or, The history of the lives, acts, death, and martyr-
  doms of . . . the primitive fathers for the first 300 years
   London, 1687 (3rd ed. corrected)
     (Binder's title: "Lives of the Fathers, Vol. I")

(129)   B55
CELLINI, Benvenuto
 Memoirs of Benvenuto Cellini, with notes of G. P. Carpani (tr.
  Thomas Roscoe)
   London, 1822 (2 vols.)

(130)   H29
CHALMERS, Alexander *editor*
    The Works of the English Poets, from Chaucer to Cowper, with
    prefaces by Dr. Samuel Johnson etc.
        London, 1810   (21 vols.)
            Vol. 3: "Spenser and Daniel"

(131)   B63
CHARDIN, *Sir* John
    Voyages du Chevalier Chardin en Perse et autres lieux de l'Orient
    (1666-1677) (nouv. éd. par L. Langlès)
        Paris, 1811   (10 vols.)

(132)   B64
CHARLES, Emile
    Roger Bacon: sa vie, ses ouvrages, ses doctrines d'après des
    textes inédits
        Paris, 1861

(133)   H47
CHARLEVOIX, Pierre François Xavier de
    Journal of a Voyage to North-America (containing a description
    of Canada etc. in letters to the Duchess of Lesdiguières)
        London, 1761   (2 vols.)

(134)   B64
CHASLES, Victor Euphémion Philarète
    Virginie de Leyva, ou Intérieur d'un couvent de Femmes en Italie
    au commencement du dix-septième siècle d'après les documents
    originaux
        Paris, 1861

(135)   B37
CHATEAUBRIAND, François Auguste René *vicomte* de
    Sketches of English Literature, with considerations on the spirit
    of the times
        London, 1836   (2 vols.)

(136)   B68
CHAUCER, Geoffrey
    The Works of Geoffrey Chaucer (three tales added by John Urry
    with a glossary by [J. Thomas] and the author's life.
        London, 1721

(137)   B42
CHEVALIER, Michel
    Society, Manners and Politics in the United States (tr. T. G.
    Bradford)
        Boston, 1839

(138)   B57
CHILD, Francis James *editor*
    English and Scottish Ballads
        Boston, 1857-1858   (8 vols.)

(139)   H46, H47
CHODZKO, Aleksander
    Specimens of the Popular Poetry of Persia
    (tr. with notes by A. C.)
        London (Oriental Translation Fund), 1842

(140)   B31
CICERO, Marcus Tullius
    Opera
        Lugd. Batav., 1642   (10 vols.)
  *Opera Omnia
        Boston, 1815   (20 vols.)

(141)   B32
CLARKSON, Thomas *clergyman*
    A Portraiture of Quakerism
        New York, 1806   (3 vols.)

(142)   B52
COBBETT, William
    Cobbett's Political Register (vols. 1-4 "Cobbett's Annual Register")
        London, 1802-1835   (88 vols.)
            Vol. 15: Jan.-June, 1809; vol. 17: Jan.-June, 1810

(143)   B51, B52
COBBETT, William; *and* T. C. Hansard *successor*
    Parliamentary Debates (vols. 1-22 ed. by Cobbett; vols. 23 and
        following by Hansard and others; still active)
        London, 1804—

(144)   B61
COCHRANE, Thomas *10th Earl of Dundonald*
    The Autobiography of a Seaman
        London, 1860   (2 vols.)

(145)   B53
COCKBURN, Henry Thomas Cockburn, *Lord*
    Life of Lord Jeffrey. With a selection from his correspondence
        Edinburgh, 1852   (2 vols.)

(146)   H26
COLERIDGE, Samuel Taylor
    Biographia Literaria, or, Biographical Sketches of my Literary
        Life and Opinions
        New York, 1817   (2 vols. in 1)

(147)   B34
COLERIDGE, Samuel Taylor
    On the Constitution of the Church and State, according to the
        idea of each
        London, 1830

(148)   B30
COLERIDGE, Samuel Taylor
    Sibylline Leaves
        London, 1817

(149)   B54
COLLINGWOOD, Cuthbert Collingwood, *1st Baron*
    Selection from the Public and Private Correspondence, with
        memoirs of his life by G. L. Newnham Collingwood
        London, 1828   (3rd ed.)

(150)   H48
COLLINS, Arthur
    Peerage of England. Greatly augmented and continued to the
        present time by Sir Egerton Brydges
            *London, 1812   (9 vols.)

(151)   B51
COLUMBUS, Christopher
    Select Letters of Christopher Columbus with other original docu-
        ments, relating to his four voyages to the new world (tr. and
        ed. by R. H. Major)
        London (Hakluyt Society), 1847

(152)   B36, B65
CONFUCIUS
    The Works of Confucius, containing the original text, with a
    translation, to which is prefixed a diss. on the Chinese language
    and character by Joshua Marshman
        Serampore, 1809   (vol. 1 all published; this contains the
        Lun-yu)

(153)   H28
COOPER, Anthony Ashley *3rd Earl of Shaftesbury*
    Characteristics of Men, Manners, Opinions, Times
        *London, 1732   (5th ed., 3 vols.)

(154)   B42
CORNEILLE, Pierre
    Le Cid, séance dramatique
        [Title-page missing. Edition uncertain.]

(155)   B68
CORNEILLE, Pierre
    Œuvres complètes, suivies des œuvres choisies
        Paris, 1838   (4 vols.)

(156)   B64
CORNHILL
    Cornhill Magazine
        London, 1860-1873   (28 vols.)

(157)   B60
COULTAS, Harland
    What May be Learned from a Tree
        New York, 1860

(158)   B72
COUSIN, Victor
    Jacqueline Pascal: Prémières études sur les femmes illustres et la
    société du XVIIe siècle
        Paris, 1856

(159)   B68
CRAIK, *Mrs.* Dinah Maria (Muloch)
    A Woman's Thoughts about Women
        London, 1858

(160)   B54
CRAIK, George Lillie
    Sketches of the history of literature and learning in England
        London, 1844-1845   (3 series in 6 vols.)
            Vol. 1: "The Norman Conquest"

(161)   B51
CUMMING [Gordon Cumming], Roualeyn Gordon
    Five Years of a Hunter's Life in the Interior of South Africa
        New York, 1850   (2 vols.)

(162)   B52
CURZON, Robert *14th baron Zouche*
    Visits to the Monasteries of the Levant
        London, 1851   (4th ed.)

D

(163)   B67
DALTON, John Call
    A Treatise on Human Physiology
        Philadelphia, 1859
        *Philadelhia, 1867   (4th ed.)

(164)   B70
DANTE ALIGHIERI
   [Opere in 6 volumes]: I-III La Divina Commedia; IV-VI Opere
   Minori
         Firenze, 1830-1841
(165)   B36
DANTE ALIGHIERI
   Vision of Hell, Purgatory, and Paradise (tr. Henry Francis
   Cary)
         London, 1819   (3 vols.)
(166)   B52
DAVIES, Edward
   The Mythology and Rites of the British Druids
         London, 1809
(167)   H26
DAVILA, Arrigo Cattarino [Enrico Caterino]
   The History of the Civil Wars of France (tr. from the Italian by
   Ellis Farneworth)
         London, 1758   (2 vols.)
(168)   B32
DAVY, *Sir* Humphry *bart.*
   Elements of Agricultural Chemistry
         New York, 1815   *[E. apparently used *copy* 1.]
(169)   H28
DAVY, *Sir* Humphry *bart.*
   Elements of Chemical Philosophy
         Philadelphia and New York, 1812 (Pt. I, Vol. 1)
(170)   B32
DAVY, *Sir* Humphry *bart.*
   Salmonia, or days of fly fishing
         London, 1829   (2nd ed.)
(171)   B55
DE LOLME, John Lewis (*or* Lolme, Jean Louis de)
   ? The Constitution of England
         Dublin, 1793   (new ed. corrected)
   ? Rise and Progress of the English Constitution (ed. A. J.
   Stephens)
         London, 1838   (2 vols.)
(172)   B58
DEMOSTHENES
   Orations (tr. Charles Rann Kennedy)
         London (Bohn), 1852-1856   (3 vols.)
(173)   B69
DIBDIN, Thomas Frognall
   Bibliomania, or, Book-madness
         *London, 1809   (1 vol.)
         *London, 1811   (1 vol.)
         London, 1829   (3 vols.)
(174)   B55
DIBDIN, Thomas Frognall
   Reminiscences of a Literary Life
         London, 1836
(175)   B62
DICEY, Edward
   Cavour: A Memoir
         Cambridge (Eng.) and London, 1861

(176)   B63
DICEY, Edward
    Six Months in the Federal States
        London and Cambridge (Eng.), 1863   (2 vols.)
(177)   B59
DIDEROT, Denis
    Mémoires, Correspondence, et Ouvrages inédits [1759-1780]
        Paris, 1830-1831   (4 vols.)
(178)   B55
DIGBY, *Sir* Kenelm
    Private Memoirs of Sir Kenelm Digby, by himself (with introd.
    by Sir Nicholas Harris Nicolas)
        London, 1827
(179)   B45
DISRAELI (D'Israeli), Isaac
    Amenities of Literature
        London, 1841   (3 vols.)
(180)   B30
DONNE, John *dean of St. Paul's Cathedral*
    Five Sermons upon Special Occasions
        London, 1626
(181)   B32
DOUCE, Francis
    Illustrations of Shakspeare and of Ancient Manners
        London, 1807   (2 vols.)
(182)   B32
DRUMMOND, James L.
    Letters to a Young Naturalist on the Study of Nature and Natural
        Theology
        London, 1831
(183)   B54
DRUMMOND, William *of Hawthornden*
    Notes of Ben Jonson's Conversations with William Drummond
    (January, 1619)
        London, 1842   (Shakespeare Society Pub. No. 8)
(184)   H23, H24
DRYDEN, John
    Miscellaneous Works, containing all his poems, tales and trans-
        lations (with his life)
        London, 1760   (4 vols.)
(185)   B70
DRYDEN, John
    Works. Illustrated with notes and a life by Walter Scott
        London, 1808   (18 vols.)
                (Vol. 17 contains "Life of Plutarch")
(186)   B64
DUCLOS, Charles Pineau
    Mémoires Secrets sur les Règnes de Louis XIV et de Louis XV
        *Paris, 1791   (2 vols.)
(187)   B45
DUCREST, Georgette
    Memoirs of the Empress Josephine, with anecdotes of the courts
        of Navarre and Malmaison
        London, 1829   (2nd ed., 3 vols.)

(188)   B62

DUDEVANT, *Mme.* Amantine Lucille Aurore Dupin (*pseud.* George Sand)
      L'Homme de Neige
           Paris, 1861   (nouv. éd., 3 vols.)

(189)   B67

DUDEVANT, *Mme.* Amantine Lucille Aurore Dupin (*pseud.* George Sand)
      Laura. Voyages et impressions
           Paris, 1865

(190)   B72

DUDEVANT, *Mme.* Amantine Lucille Aurore Dupin (*pseud.* George Sand)
      Mademoiselle Merquem
           Paris, 1870   (3ᵉ éd.)

(191)   B62

DUDEVANT, *Mme.* Amantine Lucille Aurore Dupin (*pseud.* George Sand)
      Mauprat
           Paris, 1858   (nouv. éd.)

(192)   B62

DUDEVANT, *Mme.* Amantine Lucille Aurore Dupin (*pseud.* George Sand)
      La Petite Fadette
           Paris, 1858

(193)   B65

DUDEVANT, *Mme.* Amantine Lucille Aurore Dupin (*pseud.* George Sand)
      Simon
           Paris, 1857

(194)   B54, B70

DUMONT, Pierre Etienne Louis
      Recollections of Mirabeau and of the First Legislative Assemblies of France
           Philadelphia, 1833

(195)   B34

DUPPA, Richard
      The Life of Michel Angelo Buonarroti; with his poetry and letters
           London, 1807   (2nd ed.)

(196)   B69

DWYER, *Major* Francis
      On Seats and Saddles, Bits and Bitting, and the prevention and cure of restiveness in horses
           Philadelphia, 1869

E

(197)   B31

EDINBURGH
      Edinburgh Encyclopædia (conducted by David Brewster)
           Edinburgh, 1830   (18 vols.)

(198)   H24, H25, B31, B55, B69

EDINBURGH
      Edinburgh Review
           Edinburgh, 1802-1873   (137 vols.)

(199)   B32
EDWARDS, Bryan
  The History, civil and commercial, of the British Colonies in the
    West Indies
        London, 1807   (4th ed. with additions, 3 vols.)

(200)   B32
ELEMENTS
  The Elements of Chemistry familiarly explained and prac-
    tically illustrated
        London, 1831   (Part I)

(201)   B62
ELIOT, Samuel
  History of Liberty
        Boston, 1853   (2 vols.)   (Part I: "The Ancient Romans")

(202)   B65
EMERSON, Ralph Waldo
  Poems
        Boston, 1847

(203)   B30
EMERSON, William (1769-1811)
  An Historical Sketch of the First Church in Boston, from its
    formation to the present period.   (Two sermons added)
        Boston, 1812   ("Character of Mr. Emerson" on pp. 223-
            228)   [A presentation copy from Ralph Waldo Emerson]

(204)   H18
ENCYCLOPÆDIA
  *Encyclopædia Britannica (Dobson's edn. with supplement)
        Philadelphia, 1798-1803   (21 vols.)

(205)   B32
ENCYCLOPÆDIA BRITANNICA
  Encyclopædia Britannica
        *Edinburgh, 1822-1824   (6th ed., 26 vols.)

(206)   H28
ENFIELD, William
  The History of Philosophy (drawn from Johann Brucker's *His-
    toria critica philosophiæ*
        *Dublin, 1792   (2 vols)

(207)   H47
ENGLISH POETS
  (Probably Alexander Chalmers, *The Works of the English Poets*,
    q.v. Vol. 17 of this set includes the works of Glover, White-
    head, Jago, Brooke, Scott, etc.)

(208)   B64
EPINAY, Louise Pétronille Tardieu d'Esclavelles, *marquise d'*
  Mémoires de Madame d'Epinay   (éd. nouv., avec des notes par
    Paul Boiteau)
        Paris, 1863   (2 vols.)

(209)   B69
EURIPIDES
  Tragedies (Literally tr. with notes by Theodore Alois Buckley)
        London (Bohn), 1850-1854   (2 vols.)

B31

(210)
EUSEBIUS, *Pamphili, Bp. of Caesarea in Palestine*
    The Auncient Ecclesiasticall Histories of the first six hundred
      yeares after Christ, wrytten in the Greeke tongue by . . .
      Eusebius, Socrates, and Evagrius . . . Tr. from the Greek by
      Meredith Hanmer
          [London, 1650; t.p. lacking]

B51, B54

(211)
EVELYN, John
    Diary and Correspondence [incl. private correspondence of
      Charles I, Sir Edward Nicholas, Sir Edward Hyde (Earl of
      Clarendon) and Sir Richard Browne] ed. from the original
      MSS. by William Bray
          London, 1850-1852   (new ed., 4 vols.)

B54

(212)
EVELYN, John
    The Miscellaneous Writings of John Evelyn (coll. with notes by
      W. Upcott)
          London, 1825

B37

(213)
EXAMINER
    The Examiner
          London, 1810-1871   (55 vols.)

F

B31

(214)
FABRICIUS, Johann Albert (1668-1736)
    Bibliotheca Græca, sive, Notitia scriptorum veterum Græcorum
        Hamburgi, 1718, 1716-28 (irregular)   (3rd ed., 14 vols.)

B34, B45

(215)
FAMILY
    The Family Library
        London, 1829-1842   (80 vols.)   (Issued by Murray)
    [This is to be distinguished from the *Harpers' Family Library*,
    New York, various dates (183- to 184-), 187 vols.]

        Vol.   1) Lockhart, John Gibson
              2)   The History of Napoleon Buonaparte
                  London, 1829   (2 vols.)

        Vol.   8) The Court and Camp of Buonaparte
                 London, 1831

        Vol. 33) Brewster, *Sir* David
                 Letters on Natural Magic Addressed to Sir Wal-
                 ter Scott
                 London, 1833

B45

(217)
FAUVELET DE BOURRIENNE, Louis Antoine   [Bourrienne, L. A. F.
  de]
    Private memoirs of Napoleon Bonaparte during the Directory,
      the Consulate, and the Empire
        London, 1830   (4 vols.)

B32

(218)
FEDERALIST
    Federalist: [essays] on the new Constitution [by Alexander
      Hamilton, John Jay and James Madison]
        New York, 1810   (2 vols.)
        Philadelphia, 1818   (2 vols.)

(219)   B53
FELLOWS, *Sir* Charles
        Travels and Researches in Asia Minor, more particularly in the
            Province of Lycia
                London, 1852   [Rec'd at the Athenæum, Apr. 5, 1853]
(220)   H25
FENELON, François *de Salignac de la Motte, abp. of Cambrai*
        *Œuvres de Fenelon (avec sa vie)
                Paris, 1787-1792   (9 vols.)
        Œuvres Spirituelles
                Paris, 1752   (4 vols.)
(221)   B66
FERGUSSON, James
        The Illustrated Handbook of Architecture
                London, 1855   (2 vols.)
(222)   B55
FERRIER, Susan Edmondstone [Mary]
        Destiny, or, the Chief's Daughter
                Philadelphia, 1831   (2 vols.)
(223)   B63
FICHTE, Johann Gottlieb
        The Popular Works of Johann Gottlieb Fichte
            (tr. with memoir by William Smith)
                London, 1848-1849   (2 vols.)
(224)   B66
FIELD, Henry Martyn
        History of the Atlantic Telegraph
                New York, 1866
(225)   B66
FIELD, Thomas Warren
        Pear Culture: A Manual for the propagation, planting . . . and
            management of the pear tree
                New York, 1859
(226)   H46, H47
FIRDAUSI (or Firdusi): *pseud.* of Abul Kasim Mansur
        The Sháh Námeh of the Persian Poet, Firdausi, tr. and abridged
            . . . by James Atkinson
                London, 1832   (Oriental Translation Fund, Pub. 21)
(227)   B61
FORBES, James David
        Occasional Papers on the Theory of Glaciers
                Edinburgh, 1859
(228)   B38
FOREIGN
        The Foreign Quarterly Review
                London, 1827-1846   (37 vols.)
                        (Continued as *Westminster and Foreign Quarterly
                        Review*)
(229)   B32, B34, B35
FOREIGN
        The Foreign Review, and Continental Miscellany
                London, 1828-1830   (5 vols.)

(230) B66
FORSTER, Johann Georg Adam (1754-1794)
   Sämmtliche Schriften (hrsg. von dessen Tochter und begleitet
      mit einer Charakteristik Forster's von G. G. Gervinus)
         Leipzig, 1843   (9 vols.)

(231) B45
FOUCHE, Joseph Antoine *duc d'Otrante*
   Memoirs of Joseph Fouché   (tr. from the French by E. Jules
      Méras)
         Boston and New York, 1825

(232) B35
FOX, George; *and* John Burnyeat
   A New England Fire Brand Quenched (An answer to Roger
      Williams)
         [London], 1678

(233) B32, B34, B38, B39, B56, B65
FRASER
   Fraser's Magazine
         London, 1830-1869   (First series, 80 vols.)

(234) B72
FRERE, John Hookham
   The Works of John Hookham Frere in Verse and Prose
      (With memoir by William Edward Frere and Sir Bartle Frere)
         London, 1872 [1871]   (2 vols.)
               Vol. 2: Includes translations from Aristophanes and
                  a tr. from "The Poem of the Cid" etc.

(235) B73
FROUDE, James Anthony
   The English in Ireland in the Eighteenth Century
         London, 1872-1874   (3 vols.)
         New York, 1873-1874   (3 vols.)

(236) B59
FROUDE, James Anthony
   History of England from the fall of Wolsey to the Death of
      Queen Elizabeth
         London, 1856-1870   (12 vols.)

(237) B52
FULLER, Thomas
   The History of the Worthies of England (New ed., with notes
      by John Nichols)
         London, 1811   (2 vols.)

(238) B70
FUSTEL DE COULANGES, Numa Denis
   La Cité Antique: étude sur le culte, le droit, les institutions de la
      Grèce et de Rom
         Paris, 1870   (3ᵉ édition)

G

(239) B68, B69
GARBETT, Edward Lacy
   Rudimentary Treatise on the Principles of Design in Architec-
      ture as deducible from nature and exemplified in the works of
      the Greek and Gothic Architects
         London, 1850   (2 parts in 1 vol.)
         (In John Weale's "Series of Rudimentary Works," vols.
            18-19)

(240)   B62
GASPARIN, Agénor Etienne, *comte* de
    Les Etats-Unis en 1861: Un Grand Peuple qui se relève
        Paris, 1861
(241)   B61
GASPARIN, Agénor Etienne, *comte* de
    The Uprising of a Great People: The United States in 1861 (tr.
    from the French by Mary L. Booth)
        New York, 1861
(242)   B30, B31
GERANDO, Joseph Marie de, *baron*
    Histoire Comparée des Systèmes de Philosophie
        Paris, 1804   (3 vols.)
(243)   B64
GIDDINGS, Joshua Reed
    History of the Rebellion: its authors and causes
        New York, 1864
(244)   B63, B64
GILCHRIST, Alexander
    Life of William Blake, with selections from his poems, etc., with
    a descriptive catalogue of his paintings, engravings, etc., by
    W. M. Rossetti
        London, 1863   (2 vols.)
(245)   B53
GILES, John Allen
    History of the Ancient Britons, from the earliest period to the
    invasion of the Saxons
        London, 1847   (2 vols.)
(246)   B59
GILES, John Allen
    The Life and Times of Alfred the Great
        Oxford, 1854   (2nd ed.)
(246a)   B37
GINGUENE, Pierre Louis
    Histoire Littéraire d'Italie
        Paris, 1812-1824   (10 vols.)
(247)   B66
GLADSTONE, William Ewart
    Studies on Homer and the Homeric Age
        Oxford, 1858   (3 vols.)
(248)   B64
GLADSTONE, William Ewart
    Wedgwood: an address [delivered at laying of cornerstone of
    memorial to J. Wedgwood]
        London, 1863
(249)   B32, B35
GOETHE, Johann Wolfgang von
    Memoirs of Goëthe
        New York, 1824
(250)   H49
GOETHE, Johann Wolfgang von
    Œuvres d'Histoire Naturelle . . . comprenant divers mémoires
    d'anatomie comparée, de botanique et de géologie, traduits et
    annotés par Ch. Fr. Martins
        Paris etc., 1837   [Accessioned at Harvard, Sept. 12, 1843]
            (Has a one-vol. supplementary *Atlas* by P. I. F. Turpin,
            dated at Paris and Geneva, 1837)

(251)   B61

GOETHE, Johann Wolfgang von
    Goethe's Theory of Colours (tr. with notes by Charles Lock
      Eastlake)
        London, 1840
(252)   B51

GOETHE, Johann Wolfgang von
    Goethe's Werke
        Wien, 1816-1821   (26 vols.)
(253)   H28

GOETHE, Johann Wolfgang von
    Goethe's Werke
        Stuttgart und Tübingen, 1815-1819   (20 vols.)
(254)   B32

GOETHE, Johann Wolfgang von
    Wilhelm Meister's Apprenticeship (tr. Thomas Carlyle)
        Boston, 1828   (3 vols.)
(255)   H17

GOLDSMITH, Oliver
    History of England (with continuations by M. Wood and
      Joseph McKean)
        Boston, 1814-1815   (2 vols.)   (1st American ed.)
(256)   B56

GOSSE, Philip Henry
    The Aquarium; an unveiling of the wonders of the deep sea
        London, 1854
(257)   B61

GOSSE, Philip Henry
    Letters from Alabama, chiefly relating to natural history
        London, 1859
(258)   B56

GOSSE, Philip Henry
    Tenby, a sea-side holiday
        London, 1856
(259)   B40

GRENVILLE, George Nugent-Temple, *Baron Nugent, 1st marquis of*
  Buckingham
    Some Memorials of John Hampden, his party and his times
        London, 1832   (2 vols.)
(260)   B63

GREVILLE, Fulke, *1st Baron Brooke*
    Lord Brooke's Life of Sir Philip Sidney (with preface by Sir
      Egerton Brydges)
        Kent, 1816   (2 vols.)
(261)   H48, B71

GREVILLE, Fulke, *1st Baron Brooke*
    Certaine Learned and Elegant Workes (written in his youth with
      Sir Philip Sidney)
        London, 1633
(262)   B71

GREVILLE, Fulke, *1st Baron Brooke*
    The Works in Verse and Prose complete
        (ed. with notes by Alexander B. Grosart)
          [Blackburn], 1870   (4 vols. in Fuller Worthies' Library)

(263)   B53, B54
GRIMM, Frédérich Melchior, *freiherr* von; *and* D. Diderot
    Correspondance litteraire, philosophique et critique
         Paris, 1812-1813   (3 Parts in 16 vols.)

(264)   B36
GRIMM, Jacob; *and* Wilhelm Karl Grimm
    Kinder- und Haus-Märchen
         Berlin, 1819-1822 (Zweite Auflage, 3 vols.)

(265)   B65, B66
GRIMM, Herman
    Life of Michael Angelo (tr. Fanny Elizabeth Bunnètt)
         Boston, 1865 (2 vols.)
         London, 1865 (2 vols.)

(266)   B59
GROTE, George
    A History of Greece
         London, 1846-1856 (12 vols.)

(267)   B61
GUILLIM, John
    A Display of Heraldrie
         London, 1638 (3rd ed. enlarged)

(268)   B53
GUIZOT, François Pierre Guillaume
    The History of Civilization
         New York, 1838 (1st Am. edition)

(269)   B58
GUROWSKI, Adam
    America and Europe
    New York, 1857

H

(270)   B62
HAFIZ, Muhammad Shams ad-din
    Hafis. Eine Sammlung persischer Gedichte (von G. Fr. Daumer)
         Hamburg, 1856 (2° ausg.)

(271)   HD27
HALES, John
    Golden Remains [Sermons] (with additions. Also letters con-
    cerning the Synod of Dort)
         *London, 1673 (2nd impression)

(272)   B32
HALL, *Capt.* Basil
    Fragments of Voyages and Travels
         Edinburgh, 1831-1833 (3 series in 9 vols.)

(273)   B39
HALLAM, Henry
    Introduction to the Literature of Europe in the 15th, 16th and
    17th Centuries
         London, 1837-1839 (4 vols.)

(274)   B36
HALLAM, Henry
    View of the State of Europe during the Middle Ages
         Philadelphia, 1824 (2 vols.)

(275)   H31
HAMILTON, Alexander
    The Works of Alexander Hamilton
        New York, 1810   (3 vols.)

(276)   B40
HAMILTON, Antoine *comte*
    ? Mémoires du Comte de Grammont
        Paris, 1824   (2 vols.)
    ? Memoirs of Count Grammont by Anthony Hamilton
        London, 1809   (3 vols.)
        Philadelphia, 1836   (new edition)

(277)   H25
HAMMOND, Henry
    A Paraphrase and Annotations upon all the Books of the New
        Testament
        London, 1702   (7th ed.)

(278)   B58
HAMMOND, Samuel H.
    Hills, Lakes, and Forest Streams; or a Tramp in the Chateaugay
        Woods
        New York, 1854

(279)   B70
HARDENBERG, Friedrich, *freiherr* von (*pseud.* Novalis)
    Henry of Ofterdingen: a romance from the German of Novalis
        (tr. with life of Hardenberg by Frederik S. Stallknecht)
        Cambridge (Mass.), 1842

(280)   B36, B51
HARDENBERG, Friedrich, *freiherr* von (*pseud.* Novalis)
    Novalis Schriften (hrsg. von Ludwig Tieck und Fr. Schlegel)
        Berlin, 1826   (2 vols.)   (4ᵉ aufl.)

(281)   B57
HARFORD, John Scandrett
    The Life of Michael Angelo Buonarroti; also memoirs of Savona-
        rola, Raphael and Vittoria Colonna
        London, 1857   (2 vols.)

(282)   B39
HARLEIAN
    Harleian Miscellany: or collection of scarce, curious, and enter-
        taining tracts, found in the Earl of Oxford's library, with notes
        by John Malham
        London, 1808-1811   (12 vols.)

(283)   B69
HARPER
    Harper's [New] Monthly Magazine
        New York, 1850-1875   (50 vols.)

(284)   B31
HARRINGTON, James
    The Oceana and other works (with Harrington's life by John
        Toland)
        London, 1747
        London, 1771

(285)   B30, B32, B35
HARTLEY, David
    Observations on Man, his frame, his duty, and his expectations
        London, 1801   (3 vols.)

(286)   B72
HAWEIS, Hugh Reginald
    Thought for the Times: Sermons
        New York, 1872

(287)   B55
HAY, David Ramsay
    *The Principles of Beauty in Colouring Systematized
        Edinburgh and London, 1845

(288)   B39
HAZLITT, William
    Literary Remains of the Late William Hazlitt (with thoughts on
        his genius by E. L. Bulwer and Mr. Sergeant Talfourd)
            London, 1836   (2 vols.)
                Vol. I includes "On Locke's Essay on the Human
                Understanding"

(289)   B62
HAZLITT, William
    The Round Table: a collection of essays on literature, men and
        manners
            Edinburgh, 1817   (3rd ed., 2 vols.)

(290)   B67
HAZLITT, William Carew
    Memoirs of William Hazlitt, with portions of his correspondence
        London, 1867   (2 vols.)

(291)   B65
HEGEL, Georg Wilhelm Friedrich
    Lectures on the Philosophy of History (tr. J. Sibree)
        London (Bohn), 1857

(292)   B59
HENAULT, Charles Jean François
    Abrégé Chronologique de l'histoire de France, depuis Clovis
        jusqu'à la mort de Louis XIV, continué aux 1830 par J. Michaud
            Paris, 1853   (4ᵉ édition)

(293)   B53
HENRICUS *Huntendonensis* (Henry of Huntingdon)
    The Chronicle of Henry of Huntingdon (tr. and ed., Thomas
        Forester)
            London (Bohn), 1853

(294)   B63, B68, B71
HERBERT [of Cherbury], Edward Herbert, *1st baron*
    Life of Edward Lord Herbert, of Cherbury, written by himself
        London, 1770
        *London, 1826

(295)   H29
HERDER, Johann Gottfried von
    Outlines of a Philosophy of the History of Man
        (tr. from the German by T. Churchill)
            London, 1800

(296)   B31
HERDER, Johann Gottfried von
    Outlines of a Philosophy of the History of Man
        (tr. from the German by T. Churchill)
            London, 1803   (2 vols.)

(297)   B66
HERODOTUS
    The History of Herodotus (a new English version, edited with
        notes by George Rawlinson and Sir J. G. Wilkinson)
            *London, 1858-1860   (4 vols.)

(298)   B67
HERSCHEL, *Sir* John Frederick William *bart.*
    Familiar Lectures on Scientific Subjects
            London, 1866

(299)   B64
HERVEY, John Hervey [of Ickworth], *baron*
    Memoirs of the Reign of George the Second, from his accession
        to the death of Queen Caroline (ed. by John Wilson Croker)
            London, 1848   (4 vols.)

(300)   B69
HESIODUS
    The Works of Hesiod, Callimachus and Theognis, literally tr.
        into English prose by J. Banks   (To which are added the
        metrical translations of Elton, Tytler, and Frere)
            London (Bohn), 1856

(301)   B69
HEYSE, Paul Johann Ludwig
    Vier Neue Novellen
            Berlin, 1860   (2ᵉ aufl.)

(302)   B71
HITTELL, John Shertzer
    The Resources of California (2nd ed. with an appendix on Oregon
        and Washington territory)
            San Francisco and New York, 1866

(303)   H28
HOBBES, Thomas
    [Works]   (Originally separate imprints bound in two volumes:)
    [Vol. 1]: *Dialogue on the Common Law*, London, 1681
                Considerations upon his Reputation, Religion &c., Lon-
                don, 1681
    [Vol. 2]: *Behemoth: or History of the Civil-Wars of England*,
                London, 1682

(304)   B70, B71
HOLMES, Timothy *editor*
    A System of Surgery, theoretical and practical, in treatises by
        various authors
            London, 1860-1864   (4 vols.)
                Vol. 2:   "Local Injuries. Diseases of the Eye"

(305)   B69
HOMERUS (Homer)
    [The Whole Works of Homer:] Batrachomyomachia, Hymns, and
        Epigrams etc., tr. by George Chapman, with introd. and notes
        by Richard Hooper
            London, 1858

(306)   B66
HOMERUS (Homer)
    Werke, hrsg. von Johann Heinrich Voss
            Stuttgart und Tübingen, 1821   (4 vols. in 2)

(307)   B54
HOMERUS (Homer)
    [Works] (Three different imprints bound together in one volume)
            Iliads, tr. George Chapman, London, [1611]
            Odysses, tr. George Chapman, London, [1615]
            *The Crowne of all Homer's Workes, Batrachomyo-
            machia, his Hymns and Epigrams*, tr. George Chap-
            man, London, [later than 1624]

(308)   H46
HONE, William
    Ancient Mysteries Described: esp. the English Miracle Plays
        founded on Apocryphal New Testament Story
            London, 1823

(309)   B61
HOOD, Thomas
    Prose and Verse
        New York, 1845   (2 vols.)

(310)   B54
HOOKER, Richard
    Ecclesiastical Politie
        [Edition not established]

(311)   H35
HOOKER, Richard
    Lawes of Ecclesiastical Politie (five books with discourses, ser-
        mons, etc.
            London, 1617-1631 [Bound in one volume]

(312)   H49
HOOKER, *Sir* William Jackson
    Genera Filicum; or, Illustrations of the Ferns and other allied
        genera; from the original coloured drawings of the late Francis
        Bauer . . . with additions
            London, 1842

(313)   B62
HOPE, Thomas
    Costume of the Ancients
        London, 1841   (new edition, 2 vols.)

(314)   B71
HORATIUS FLACCUS, Quintus
    Opera Omnia, ed. Godofredus Stallbaum
        Lipsiæ, 1854

(315)   B30
HOWELL, James
    Epistolæ Ho-Elianæ: familiar letters, domestic and forren (*sic*)
        London, 1673   (4th edition)

(316)   B31
HOYT, Epaphras
    Antiquarian Researches, comprising a history of the Indian Wars
        Greenfield (Mass.), 1824

(317)   B32
HUBER, François
    New Observations on the Natural History of Bees
        Edinburgh, 1821   (3rd edition)

(318)   B32

HUBER, Pierre (*i.e.,* Jean Pierre)
    The Natural History of Ants (tr. from the French, with notes
        by J. R. Johnson)
            London, 1820
(319)   B70

HUFELAND, Christoph Wilhelm
    The Art of Prolonging Life
            London, 1797   (2 vols.)
(320)   B67

HUGO, Victor Marie, *comte*
    Les Chansons des Rues et des Bois
            Paris, 1866   (2° édition)
(321)   B60

HUMBOLDT, Alexander, *freiherr* von
    *Letters to Varnhagen von Ense. From 1827 to 1858. With ex-
        tracts from Varnhagen's diaries and letters of Varnhagen and
        others to Humboldt (tr. from 2nd German ed. by Friedrich
        Kapp)
            New York, 1860
(322)   H25

HUME, David
    Essays and Treatises on Several Subjects
            *London, 1768   (2 vols.)
            Basil, 1793   (4 vols.)
(323)   H18, H25

HUME, David
    The History of England
            *Philadelphia, etc., 1810   (7 vols.)
(324)   B35

HUTCHINSON, Thomas
    A Collection of Original Papers relative to the history of the
        Colony of Massachusetts Bay
            Boston, 1769
(325)   H29

HUTCHINSON, Thomas
    The History of Massachusetts
            *Boston, 1795-1828   (3 vols.)
(326)   B70

HUXLEY, Thomas Henry
    Lay Sermons, Addresses, and Reviews
            London, 1870

I

(327)   B58

ILLUSTRATED
    The Illustrated London News
            London, 1842-1875   (67 vols.)

J

(328)   B37

JACOBI, Friedrich Heinrich
    Friedrich Heinrich Jacobi's Werke
            Leipzig, 1812-1825   (6 vols. in 8)

(329)   B61
JALAL-AD-DIN
        Auswahl aus den Diwanen des grössten mystischen Dichters
        Persiens Mewlana Dschelaleddin Rumi aus dem Persischen
        mit beigefügtem original-texte und erläternden Anmerkungen
        von Vicenz von Rosenzweig
                Vienna, 1838

(330)   H47, B72
JAMIESON, Robert *editor*
        Popular Ballads and Songs from Tradition, Manuscripts and
        Scarce Editions
                Edinburgh, 1806   (2 vols.)

(331)   B34
JAY, William (1789-1858)
        The Life of John Jay: with selections from his correspondence
        and miscellaneous papers
                New York, 1833   (2 vols.)

(332)   B32
JEFFERYS, Thomas
        A Description of the Spanish Islands and Settlements on the
        Coast of the West Indies (with maps)
                *London, 1762

(333)   B52
JESSE, John Heneage
        George Selwyn and his Contemporaries, with memoirs and notes
                London, 1843-1844   (4 vols.)

(334)   H18, H28
JOHNSON, Samuel
        Works (with Life and notes on his *Lives of the Poets* by Sir
        John Hawkins)
                London, 1787-1788   (14 vols.)

(335)   B52
JOHNSTON, William
        England As it Is, Political, Social and Industrial, in the middle
        of the Nineteenth Century
                London, 1851   (2 vols.)

(336)   B54
JONES, John (1774-   )
        Attempts in Verse by John Jones, an old Servant, with some
        account of the writer, written by himself: and an introductory
        essay on the lives and works of our uneducated poets by Robert
        Southey
                London, 1831

(337)   B40
JONES, *Sir* William (1746-1794)
        Works
                London, 1799   (6 vols.)

(338)   H23, H26, H28
JONSON, Ben
        Works (ed. with notes by Peter Whalley)
                London, 1756   (7 vols.)

(339)   B45
JOURNAL
        Journal of the Academy of Natural Sciences of Philadelphia
                Philadelphia, 1817-1830   (6 vols.)

(340)   B40, B42
JUNOT, Laure (Permon), *duchesse d'Abrantès*
    Memoirs [in English]
        Paris, 1831-1835   (8 vols.)

(341)   B64
JUVENALIS, Decimus Junius
    The Satires of Juvenal, Persius, Sulpicia, and Lucilius literally
        tr. by Lewis Evans, with metrical version of Juvenal and
        Persius, by William Gifford
        London (Bohn), 1852

K

(342)   B64
KARR, [Jean Baptiste] Alphonse
    A Tour Round My Garden (ed. J. G. Wood)
        London, 1856

(343)   B68, B70
KAVANAGH, Julia
    Adèle: A Tale
        New York, 1858

(344)   B52
KEMBLE, John Mitchell
    The Saxons in England (until the Norman Conquest)
        London, 1849   (2 vols.)

(345)   B30, B31
KIRBY, William; *and* William Spence
    An Introduction to Entomology
        London, 1816-1826   (Parts of two editions: 4 vols.)

(346)   B32
KNAPP, John Leonard
    The Journal of a Naturalist
        London, 1829

(347)   B65, B66
KNIGHT, Charles
    The Popular History of England
        London, 1856-1862   (8 vols.)

(348)   B54
KNOWLES, John *editor*
    Life and Writings of Henry Fuseli, the former written and the
        latter edited by, John Knowles
        London, 1831

L

(349)   B35
LAMB, Charles
    ? Elia: essays which have appeared . . . in the London Magazine
        London, 1823   (1st edition)
    ? Last Essays of Elia; being a sequel to "Essays"
        London, 1833   (1st edition)

(350)   B32
LAMB, Charles
    Works
        London, 1818   (1st ed., 2 vols.)

(351)   B64
LANDOR, Walter Savage
   Heroic Idyls, with additional poems
      London, 1863

(352)   B31, B32
LANDOR, Walter Savage
   Imaginary Conversations of Literary Men and Statesmen
      London, 1826-1829   (2nd ed., enlarged, 5 vols.)

(353)   B32, B35, B45
LANDOR, Walter Savage
   Imaginary Conversations of Literary Men and Statemen
   (SECOND SERIES)
      London, 1829   (2 vols.)

(354)   B70
LANFREY, Pierre
   Histoire de Napoléon Ier
      Paris, 1869-1875   (5 vols.)

(355)   B32, B34, B37, B38, B39
LARDNER, Dionysius
   The Cabinet Cyclopædia
      London, 1830-1846   (133 vols.)

   (The volume numbers given below are those of the Athenæum
   and not the official numbers of the volumes as published. From
   all indications, the Athenæum arrangement has not been
   changed since Emerson's day. For complete list, see the *Catalogue*, 1874-1880.)

Vols.   (356)
17-19)   Gleig, George Robert
      Eminent British Military Commanders
         London, 1831-1832   (3 vols.)   [Vol. 19 (1832)]

       (357)
34-38)   Crowe, Eyre Evans; *and* G. P. R. James
      Eminent Foreign Statesmen
         London, 1833-1838   (5 vols.)   [Vol. 34 (1834)]

       (358)
62-64)   Dunham, Samuel Astley
      History of the Germanic Empire
         London, 1834-1835   (3 vols.)

       (359)
67-74)   Thirlwall, Connop *bp. of St. David's*
      A History of Greece
         London, 1835-1844   (8 vols.)

       (360)
80-82)   Cooley, William Desborough
      History of Maritime and Inland Discovery
         London, 1830-1831   (3 vols.)

       (361)
84)   Keightley, Thomas
      Outlines of History
         London, 1830

(362)
90-91)   Bell, Robert
             History of Rome
                   London, [1839] (new ed., 2 vols.)

(363)
92-94)   Bell, Robert
             A History of Russia
                   London, 1836-1838   (3 vols.)

(364)
95-96)   Scott, Sir Walter
             The History of Scotland
                   London, 1830   (2 vols.)

(365)
97-101)   Dunham, Samuel Astley
             History of Spain and Portugal
                   London, 1832-1833   (5 vols.)

(366)
108)   Swainson, William
             Animals in Menageries
                   London, 1838

(367)
112-113) Swainson, William
             On the Natural History and Classification of Fishes,
                Amphibians, and Reptiles
                   London, 1838-1839   (2 vols.)

(368)
114-115) Phillips, John
             Treatise on Geology
                   London, 1837-1839   (2 vols.)

(369)   HD29, B31
LARDNER, Nathaniel
       Works: containing Credibility of the Gospel History, Jewish and
          Heathen Testimonies; History of Heretics. With life of the
          author by Andrew Kippis
             London, 1788   (11 vols.)

(370)   B69
LAYARD, Sir Austen Henry
       Ninevah and its Remains: A narrative of an expedition (1845-
          1847)
             London, 1867   (abridged edition)

(371)   H47
LAYS
       Lays of the Minnesingers; or German troubadours of the 12th
          and 13th Centuries (ed. Edgar Taylor)
             London, 1825

(372)   B67
LEGGE, James
       The Chinese Classics, with a translation, notes, etc.
             London, 1862-1865 (Athenæum has only 3 vols. in 4 parts)
                Vol. 2: Works of Mencius

(373)   H25
LEIBNITZ (Leibniz), Gottfried Wilhelm, freiherr von
       Essais de Theodicée sur la Bonté de Dieu, la Liberté d'homme
          et l'Origine du Mal
             Amsterdam, 1710

(374)　　　　　　　　　　　　　　　　　　　　　　B65, B66
LESLIE, Charles Robert; *and* Tom Taylor
　　Life and Times of Sir Joshua Reynolds
　　　　London, 1865　(2 vols.)

(375)　　　　　　　　　　　　　　　　　　　　　　B32
LESLIE, *Sir* John
　　Elements of Natural Philosophy
　　　　Edinburgh, 1823　(Vol. 1 only)

(376)　　　　　　　　　　　　　　　　　　　　　　B67
LESSING, Gotthold Ephraim
　　Sämmtliche Schriften
　　　　Berlin, 1784-1824　(30 vols.)
　　　　　　Vol.　3: Rettung des Lemnius—des Cochläus—des
　　　　　　　　　H. Cardanus—des Inepti religiosi—Rettun-
　　　　　　　　　gen des Horaz
　　　　　　Vol. 10: Laokoon etc.

(377)　　　　　　　　　　　　　　　　　　　　　　B70
LEWES, George Henry
　　The Life and Works of Goethe
　　　　Boston, 1856　(2 vols.)

(378)　　　　　　　　　　　　　　　　　　　　　　B30
LEWIS, Matthew Gregory *author and collector*
　　Tales of Wonder
　　　　New York, 1801　(2 vols.)

(379)　　　　　　　　　　　　　　　　　　　　　　B54
LIEBER, Francis
　　Manual of Political Ethics
　　　　Boston, 1838-1839　(2 vols.)

(380)　　　　　　　　　　　　　　　　　　　　　　B64
LIEBER, Francis
　　Reminiscences of an Intercourse with [George Berthold]
　　　　Niebuhr (in Rome, 1822-1823)
　　　　　　Philadelphia, 1835

(381)　　　　　　　　　　　　　　　　B39, B57, B58
LINNÆUS (Linné), Carl von
　　Lachesis Lapponica, or A Tour in Lapland (ed. James Edward
　　　　Smith)
　　　　　　London, 1811　(2 vols.)

(382)　　　　　　　　　　　　　　　　　　　　　　B45
LITERARY AND PHILOSOPHICAL SOCIETY
　　Transactions of the Literary and Philosophical Society of New
　　　　York
　　　　　　New York, 1815　(vol. 1)

(383)　　　　　　　　　　　　　　　　　　　　　　H28
LOCKE, John
　　*Familiar Letters Between Mr. Locke and Several of his Friends,
　　　　with his life and character
　　　　　　London, 1742　(4th edition)

(384)　　　　　　　　　　　　　　　　　　　　　　B58
LOCKHART, John Gibson *translator*
　　Ancient Spanish Ballads, historical and romantic
　　　　London, 1823

(385) B57

LOMENIE, Louis Léonard de
    Beaumarchais and his Times: Sketches of French Society in the
        Eighteenth Century. Tr. Henry S. Edwards
            London, 1856   (4 vols.)

(386) B34

LONDON
    The London Journal of Arts, Sciences and Manufactures
        (THIRD or Conjoined Series)
            London, 1832-1854   (45 vols.)
                [The earlier series were:
                    First: London, 1820-1828 (14 vols.)
                    Second: London, 1828-1834 (19 vols.)

(387) B69

LONGMAN, William
    The History of the Life and Time of Edward III
            London, 1869   (2 vols.)

(388) B57

LOOMIS, Elias
    The Recent Progress of Astronomy, especially in the United
        States
            New York, 1856   (3rd edition enlarged)

(389) B61

LORING, James Spear
    The Hundred Boston Orators, appointed by the Municipal Au-
        thorities and other Public Societies from 1770 to 1852
            Boston, 1852

(390) B72

LOWELL, James Russell
    *Poetical Works
            Boston, 1871   (2 vols.)

(391) H48

LOWTH, Robert, *bishop of London*
    The Life of William of Wykeham, Bishop of Winchester
            London, 1759   (2nd edition)

(392) B69

LUBBOCK, *Sir* John, *1st baron Avebury*
    Pre-historic Times, as illustrated by ancient remains and the
        manners and customs of modern savages
            London, 1865   (1st edition)
            London, 1869   (2nd edition)

(393) B32

LUCAS, Richard
    Practical Christianity; or, An account of the holiness which the
        Gospel enjoins, with the motives to it, and the remedies it
        proposes against temptations . . .
            London, 1708   (6th edition)

(394) B34

LUTHER, Martin
    A Commentary upon the Epistle to the Galatians
            [London, 1635? Title-page is missing.]

(395)   B52
LUTHER, Martin
  Life. Written by himself; collected and arranged (with additions)
   by M. Michelet; tr. by William Hazlitt
    London, 1846   (Bogue's European Library)
(396)   B36
LYELL, *Sir* Charles, *1st bart.*
  Principles of Geology
    London, 1830-1833   (2nd ed., 3 vols.)
(397)   B70
LYRA
  Lyra Apostolica: [Poems by J. W. Bowden, R. H. Froude, John
   Keble, J. H. Newman, R. I. Wilberforce, and I. Williams]
    London, 1864   (13th edition)
(398)   B42
LYTTON, Edward George Earle Lytton Bulwer, *1st baron* (*pseud.*
Pisistratus Caxton)
  Alice; or the Mysteries: a sequel to *Ernest Maltravers*
   New York (Harpers), 1838   (2 vols.)
(399)   B42
LYTTON, Edward George Earle Lytton Bulwer, *1st baron* (*pseud.*
Pisistratus Caxton)
  Ernest Maltravers
   New York, 1837   (2 vols.)
(400)   B66
LYTTON, Edward George Earle Lytton Bulwer, *1st baron* (*pseud.*
Pisistratus Caxton)
  The Lost Tales of Miletus
   London, 1866

M

(401)   H55, B58, B60, B61, B63, B72
MABINOGION
  The Mabinogion. From the Llyfr Coch o Hergest, and other
   ancient Welsh manuscripts, with an English translation and
   notes by Lady Charlotte E. Guest
    London, 1849   (3 vols.)
(402)   B53
MACAULAY, Thomas Babington, *1st Baron*
  Speeches by the Rt. Hon. Thomas Babington Macaulay
   New York, 1853   (2 vols.)
(403)   B64
MACMILLAN
  Macmillan's Magazine
  London, 1860-1877   (30 vols.)
(404)   B64
MACPHERSON, James
  An Original Collection of the Poems of Ossian, Orrann, Ulin,
   and other bards (ed. by H. and J. McCallum)
    Montrose, 1816
(405)   B61
McCLINTOCK, *Sir* [Francis] Leopold
  The Voyage of the 'Fox' in the Arctic Seas. A narrative of the
   discovery of the fate of Sir John Franklin and his companions
    Boston, 1860

(406)   B72
McCRIE, Thomas
    The Life of John Knox, containing illustrations of the Reforma-
    tion in Scotland
        Edinburgh, 1818   (4th ed., 2 vols.)

(407)   B55
MADDEN, Richard Robert
    The Literary Life and Correspondence of the Countess of
    Blessington
        New York, 1855   (2 vols.)

(408)   B63
MAGASIN
    Magasin Encyclopédique, ou Journal des sciences, des lettres
    et des arts (redigé par A. L. Millin)
        Paris, 1795-1809   (84 vols.)   (Six vols. were issued an-
        nually)

(409)   B54
MAHAWANSO (or Mahānāma or Maha Naama)
    The Maháwanso, in Roman characters, with the translation,
    and an essay on Páli Buddhistical literature, by G. Turnour
        Ceylon, 1837   (vol. 1 all published)

(410)   B64
MALCOLM, Sir John
    The History of Persia
        London, 1815   (2 vols.)
        London, 1829   (2 vols.)

(411)   H47
MALLET, Paul Henri
    Northern Antiquities, or a description of the manners, customs
    etc. of the ancient Danes, with a translation of the Edda;
    (Tr. from the French of Mallet by Bishop [Thomas] Percy;
    notes added by I. A. Blackwell. An abstract of the "Eyrbyggja
    Saga" by Sir Walter Scott
        London (Bohn), 1847

(412)   B60
MALORY, Sir Thomas
    The Byrth, Lyf, and Actes of Kyng Arthur . . . thachyevyng of
    the Sanc Greal and . . . le Morte Darthur (with introd. and
    notes by Robert Southey)   [Caxton's edition, 1485]
        London, 1817   (2 vols.)

(413)   B69
MARSH, George Perkins
    Man and Nature, or, Physical Geography as modified by human
    action
        New York, 1864
        (Later pub. with title: *The Earth as Modified by Human
        Action*)

(414)   H31
MARSH, Herbert, *bishop of Peterborough* (translator)
    Introduction to the New Testament [by Johann David Michaelis]
    tr. from the 4th German ed., and augmented with notes and a
    diss. on the origin and composition of the first three gospels,
    by Herbert Marsh
        London, 1802   (2nd ed., 4 vols.)

(415)   B67
MARSHMAN, John Clark
    The History of India (to the close of Lord Dalhousie's adminis-
    tration)
            London, 1867   (3 vols.)

(416)   B30
MASSACHUSETTS
    (The charging list reads either "Mass. Comm" or "Mass. Laws,"
    182[?]. The present editor cannot identify it. Possibly *General
    Laws*, Boston, 1823 (2 vols.) or *Special Laws*, Boston, 1805-
    1823 (5 vols.)

(417)   H35, B69
MASSACHUSETTS HISTORICAL SOCIETY
    Collections of the Massachusetts Historical Society
            Boston, 1795-1816 (10 vols.)   (FIRST SERIES)
            Boston, 1814-1823 (10 vols.)   (SECOND SERIES)
                (Athenæum has 43 vols., Boston, 1795-1877)

                        (418)
        II.5)   Hubbard, William
        or   General History of New England (1620-1680)
        15)   Boston, 1815

                        (419)
        IV.3)   Bradford, William
        or   History of Plymouth Plantation
        33)   Boston, 1856   (See *supra*)

(420)   B68
MASSACHUSETTS QUARTERLY
    Massachusetts Quarterly Review
            Boston, 1847-1850   (all published)   (3 vols.)

(421)   B59
MASSON, David
    Essays, biographical and critical: chiefly on English Poets
            Cambridge (Mass.), 1856

(422)   B61
MATHER, Cotton
    Magnalia Christi Americani: or, The ecclesiastical history of
    New-England (1620-1698)
            London, 1702

(423)   B32
MAWE, John
    The Linnæan System of Conchology
            London, 1823

(424)   B34, B35
MAYO, Charles (1792-1846)
    Memoir of Pestalozzi, being the substance of a lecture delivered,
    May, 1826
            London, 1828

(425)   B57
MECHANICS
    The Mechanics' Magazine and Journal of Science, Arts, and
    Manufactures
            London, 1823-1858   (69 vols.)

(426) B52
MEDWIN, Thomas
The Life of Percy Bysshe Shelley
London, 1847 (2 vols.)

(427) B66
METEYARD, Eliza
The Life of Josiah Wedgwood (with sketch of the art of pottery
in England)
London, 1865-1866 (2 vols.)

(428) B40
MICHAUX, François André
Histoire des Chênes de l'Amérique, ou descriptions et figures de
toutes les espèces et variétés de chênes de l'Amerique Sep-
tentrionale, considérées sous les rapports de la botanique, de
leur culture et de leur usage
Paris, 1801

(429) B65, B66
MICHELET, Jules
Histoire de France
Paris, 1833-1866 (16 vols.)

(430) H26
MIDDLETON, Conyers
The Life of Marcus Tullius Cicero
*London, 1801 (new ed., 3 vols.)

(431) B40
MIGNAN, Robert
Travels in Chaldæa (including journey on foot to Bagdad, Hillah
and Babylon in 1827, with observations on the sites and re-
mains of Babel, Seleucia and Ctesiphon)
London, 1829

(432) B35
MILNER, Joseph; and Isaac Milner
History of the Church of Christ
Boston, 1809-1811 (4 vols. in 5 parts)

(433) HD28
MILTON, John
The Poetical Works of John Milton (with notes of various com-
mentators, and his life by Henry Todd)
*London, 1801 (6 vols.)

(434) B35, B36
MILTON, John
Prose Works, with life, translations, and critical remarks by
C. Symmons
London, 1806 (7 vols.)

(435) HD29
MILTON, John
A Selection from the English Prose Works (ed. Francis Jenks)
Boston, 1826 (2 vols.)
Binder's Title: "Prose Works"

(436) B53
MIRABEAU, Honoré Gabriel Riguetti, comte de
Mirabeau's Letters during his Residence in England (with notes
on his life, writings and character)
London, 1832 (2 vols.)

(437)   H24, H25, H26
MITFORD, William
    The History of Greece
        London, 1795-1797.   (6 vols.)
        Boston, 1823   (8 vols.)

(438)   B64
MOHL, Mary (Clarke)
    Madame Récamier; with a sketch of the history of society in
      France
        London, 1862

(439)   B62, B65
MOMMSEN, Theodor
    The History of Rome (tr. W. P. Dickson)
        London, 1862-1866   (4 vols. in 5 parts)

(440)   B55
MONTAGU, *Lady* Mary Wortley
    The Letters and Works   (ed. Lord Wharncliffe)
        London, 1837   (3 vols.)
        Paris, 1837   (2 vols.)

(441)   H23, H26, H27
MONTAIGNE, Michel de
    The Essays of Michael Seigneur de Montaigne
    (tr. from the French ed. of Peter Coste)
        London, 1759   (7th ed., 3 vols.)

(442)   B63
MONTLUC, Blaise [de Lasseran-Massencome, *seigneur*] de
    The Commentaries of Messire Blaize de Montluc, Mareschal of
      France
        London, 1674

(443)   B63
MOODY, Charles Cotesworth Pinckney
    Biographical Sketches of the Moody Family (1633-1642)
        Boston, 1847

(444)   B51
MOORE, Thomas
    Letters and Journals of Lord Byron; with notices of his life
        London, 1830   (2 vols.)

(445)   B53, B55
MOORE, Thomas
    Memoirs, Journal, and Correspondence of Thomas Moore
    (ed. Lord John Russell)
        London, 1853-1856   (8 vols.)

(446)   B35
MOORE, Thomas
    Memoirs of the Life of the Rt. Hon. Richard Brinsley Sheridan
        Philadelphia, 1825
(447)   B55
MOORE, Thomas
    Notes from the Letters of Thomas Moore to his Music Publisher,
    James Power (with introd. letter from Thomas Crofton Croker)
        New York, [1854]   (Publication of these was suppressed
        in London)

(448)   B30

MORE, Henry
    Divine Dialogues, containing sundry disquisitions & instructions
       concerning the attributes of God and his Providence in the
       world (collected and compiled by Franciscus Palaeopolitanus)
           London, 1668

(449)   B68

MORLEY, Henry *editor*
    The King and the Commons: Cavalier and Puritan songs
           London, 1868

(450)   H23, B31

MOSHEIM, Johann Lorenz von
    An Ecclesiastical History, antient and modern
       (tr. Archibald Maclaine)
          *Charlestown (Mass.), 1810-1811 (6 vols.) (This edition
            contains a vindication of the Quakers by J. G. Bevan)

(451)   B68

MUELLER (Müller), Friedrich Max
    Chips from a German Workshop
           London, 1867-1875 (4 vols.)

(452)   B61

MUELLER, (Müller), Friedrich Max
    A History of Ancient Sanskrit Literature, so far as it illustrates
       the primitive religion of the Brahmins
           London, 1860 (2nd ed.)

(453)   B62, B67

MUELLER, (Müller), Friedrich Max
    Lectures on the Science of Language
           London, 1861-1864 (1st and 2nd series, 2 vols.)

(454)   B72

MUELLER, (Müller), Friedrich Max
    Lectures on the Science of Religion; with a paper on Buddhist
       nihilism, and a translation of the Dhammapada or "Path of
       Virtue"
           New York, 1872

(455)   B31

MUELLER (Müller), Karl Otfried
    History and Antiquities of the Doric Race (tr. Henry Tufnell
       and George Cornewall Lewis)
           Oxford, 1830 (2 vols.)

(456)   B63

MURGER, Henry
    Adeline Protat [Scènes de Campagne]
          Paris, 1862 (This is vol. 4 of *Œuvres Complètes*)

(457)   B71

MURGER, Henry
    Le Sabot Rouge
          Paris, 1861 (2ᵉ édition) (Vol. 8 of *Œuvres Complètes*)

(458)   B36

MUSAEUS (Musäus), Johann Karl August
    Volksmärchen der Deutschen; mit einem Vorwort von Frederich
       Jacobs
           Gotha, 1826 (neue Auflage, 5 vols.)

N

(459)   B45

NAPOLEON I, *Emperor of the French*
  Memoirs of the History of France (Historical Miscellanies)
      London, 1823 (3 vols.)

(460)   B32

NEW
  New Monthly Magazine
      London, 1814-1867   (153 vols.)

(461)   H25

NEWTON, *Sir* Isaac
  The Chronology of Antient Kingdoms Amended (To the con-
      quest of Persia by Alexander the Great)
      *Dublin, 1728

(462)   H55

NIEBUHR, Barthold Georg
  Lectures on Ancient Ethnography and Geography (tr. from
      German ed. of Dr. Isler by Leonhard Schmitz)
      *Boston, 1854   (2 vols.)

(463)   H55, B55

NIEBUHR, Barthold Georg
  Lectures on the History of Rome (ed. Leonhard Schmitz)
      *London, 1849   (3 vols.)
      London, 1852   (3 vols.)

(464)   B55, H55

NIEBUHR, Barthold Georg
  The Life and Letters of Barthold George Niebuhr; with essays
      on his character and influence by [Baron] Bunsen, [Johannes]
      Brandis, and [Johann Wilhelm] Loebell
      London, 1852   (3 vols.)

(465)   B32

NITSCH, F. A.
  A General and Introductory View of Professor Kant's Principles
      concerning man, the world, and the deity
      London, 1796

(466)   B61

NJALA [Njals Saga]
  The Story of Burnt Njal: or Life in Iceland at the end of the
      Tenth Century (tr. from the Icelandic by George Webbe
      Dasent)
      Edinburgh, 1861   (2 vols.)

(467)   H32

NORTH, Roger
  Examen: or, An Enquiry into the Credit and Veracity of a Pre-
      tended Complete History [Kennet's] (with Memoirs tending to
      vindicate Charles II.)
      London, 1740

(468)   B32

NORTH, Roger
  The Lives of the Rt. Hon. Francis North, baron Guilford, Sir
      Dudley North, . . . and the Rev. Dr. John North
      London, 1826   (new edition, 3 vols.)

(469)   B67

NORTH AMERICAN
  North American Review
      Boston, 1815-1876   (123 vols.)

O

(470)   B40, B42

OCKLEY, Simon
  The Conquest of Syria, Persia and Ægypt by the Saracens
          London, 1708-1718   (2 vols.)
          (Note: vol. 2 is entitled "History of the Saracens")

(471)   B60

OLIPHANT, Laurence
  Narrative of the Earl of Elgin's Mission to China and Japan
      (1857-1859)
          Edinburgh and London, 1859   (2 vols.)

(472)   B70

OLIVER, Peter
  The Puritan Commonwealth: An historical review of the Puritan
      government in Massachusetts (with reflections on English
      colonial policy)
          Boston, 1856

(473)   B60, B68

OWEN, Sir Richard
  Palæontology: or, A systematic summary of extinct animals in
      their geological relations
          London, 1860

(474)   H47

OZANAM, Antoine Frédéric
  Dante et la Philosophie Catholique au Treizième Siècle
          Paris, 1839
          Paris, 1840
          Paris, 1845

P

(475)   B31

PALEY, William
  A View of the Evidences of Christianity
          Dublin, 1794   (2nd edition)
          Philadelphia, 1795

(476)   B67

PALGRAVE, Francis Turner
  Essays on Art
          London and Cambridge, 1866

(477)   B67

PALGRAVE, William Gifford
  Narrative of a Year's Journey through Central and Eastern
      Arabia (1862-1863)
          London and Cambridge, 1865   (2 vols.)
          London and Cambridge, 1866   (2 vols.)

(478)   B32

PARIS, John Ayrton
  The Life of Sir Humphry Davy, Bart.
          London, 1831

(479)   B32

PARIS [France]: Académie des Inscriptions et Belles Lettres
  Histoire de l'Académie etc. . . . avec les mémoires de Lit-
      térature (1701-1793)
          Paris, 1736-1808   (50 vols.)

(480)   B69
PARLIAMENTARY
    Parliamentary History of England, by several hands
    [1106-1660]
            London, 1762-1763   (23 vols.)

(481)   B30
PARRY, *Sir* William Edward
    Journal of a Second Voyage for the Discovery of a North-West
    Passage from the Atlantic to the Pacific (1821-1823 in
    H. M. S. "Fury" and "Hecla")
            London, 1824

(482)   B30
PARRY, *Sir* William Edward
    Journal of a Third Voyage for the Discovery of a North-West
    Passage from the Atlantic to the Pacific (1824-1825 in
    H. M. S. "Hecla" and "Fury")
            London, 1826
            Philadelphia, 1826

(483)   B72
PATIN, Henri Joseph Guillaume
    Études sur la Poésie Latine
            Paris, 1868   (2 vols.)

(484)   B57
PAYEN, Jean François *editor*
    Documents inédits ou peu connus sur Montaigne
            Paris, 1847

(485)   H46
PELET DE LA LOZERE, [Privat Joseph Claramond] *comte*
    Napoleon in Council, or, The Opinions delivered by Bonaparte
    in the Council of State (tr. Capt. Basil Hall)
            Edinburgh and London, 1837

(486)   B30, B32, B35
PENN, William
    The Select Works of William Penn
            London, 1782   (3rd ed., 5 vols.)

(487)   B38, B54
PEPYS, Samuel
    Memoirs: comprising his dairy from 1659-1669, deciphered by
    John Smith and edited by Richard Lord Braybrooke
            *London, 1825   (2 vols.)   B38
            London, 1851   (4 vols.)

(488)   B42, B45
PERCY, Thomas, *bishop of Dromore*
    Reliques of Ancient English Poetry
            London, 1794   (3 vols., 4th edition)
            London, 1812   (3 vols.)

(489)   B61, B62
PETITOT, Claude Bernard
    Collection complète des Mémoires relatifs à l'Histoire de France
            Paris, 1819-1827   (1° ser.)   (52 vols.)
            Paris, 1820-1829   (2° ser.)   (78 vols.)

(490)   B70
PHELPS, Elizabeth Stuart (*Mrs*. H. D. Ward)
    Hedged In
            Boston, 1870

(491)   B42
PHILOSOPHICAL MAGAZINE
    London, Edinburgh, and Dublin Philosophical Magazine and
        Journal of Science
            London, 1798-1826   (68 vols.)
(492)   B58
PHIPPS, Constantine Henry, *1st Marquis of Normanby*
    A Year of Revolution. From a Journal kept in Paris in 1848
            London, 1857   (2 vols.)
(493)   B70
PINDARUS
    Carmina et Fragmenta cum Lectionis varietate et Annotationibus
        a C. G. Heyne
            Oxonii, 1807   (2 vols.)
(494)   B59
PIOZZI, *Mrs.* Hester Lynch (Salusbury) Thrale
    Anecdotes of the late Samuel Johnson
            London, 1786   (4th edition)
(495)   H46
PLATO
    Platons Werke   (ed. Friedrich Schleiermacher)
            Berlin, 1804-1809   (5 bde.)
(496)   H26, H27, H29, B30, B31, B36, B39, B42, B45
PLATO
    The Works of Plato: viz, his fifty-five dialogues and twelve
        epistles, tr. from the Greek; nine dialogues by the late Floyer
        Sydenham, and the remainder by Thomas Taylor: with occa-
        sional annotations . . . in which is given the substance of
        nearly all the existing Greek manuscript commentaries on the
        philosophy of Plato, and a considerable portion of such as are
        already published
            London, 1804   (5 vols.)
(497)   B34
PLAYFAIR, John
    The Works of John Playfair (with memoir)
            Edinburgh, 1822   (4 vols.)
(498)   H26, H27, H28
PLUTARCHUS
    Œuvres de Plutarque (trad. du Grec par Jacques Amyot avec
        des Notes par Brotier)
            Paris, 1783-1787   (22 vols.)
(499)   H25
POPE, Alexander
    Works (with notes and illustrations by Joseph Warton and others)
            *London, 1797   (9 vols.)
(500)   H29
PORSON, Richard
    Letters to Archdeacon Travis, in Answer to his Defence of the
        Three Heavenly Witnesses (*1 John* V.7)
            London, 1790
(501)   B53
PORTER, George Richardson
    The Progress of the Nation, in its various social and economical
        relations, from the beginning of the Nineteenth Century
            London, 1836-1838   (3 vols.)
            *London, 1851   (new edition)

(502)   B65
PRAED, Winthrop Mackworth
    The Poems of Winthrop Mackworth Praed (with memoir by the
      Rev. Derwent Coleridge)
          London, 1864   (2nd ed., 2 vols.)

(503)   H68
PRELLER, Ludwig
    ? Die Regionem der Stadt Rom
          Jena, 1846   (Acquired by Harvard, Nov. 15, 1861)
    ? Römische Mythologie
          Berlin, 1858   (Acquired by Harvard, June 25, 1860)
    ? Ausgewählte Aufsätze aus dem Gebiete der classischen Alter-
      thumswissenschaft (hrsg. Reinhold Köhler)
          Berlin, 1864   (Acquired by Harvard, Dec. 18, 1866)

(504)   B55
PRICHARD, James Cowles
    The Natural History of Man; comprising inquiries into the
      modifying influence of physical and moral agencies on the
      different tribes of the human family
          London, 1843

(505)   H18
PRIESTLEY, Joseph
    Lectures on History and General Policy (with an essay on a
      course of education for civil and active life)
          Dublin, 1791   (3rd edition)
          London, 1793   (2 vols.)
          *Philadelphia, 1803   (2 vols.)

(506)   H24
PRIESTLEY, Joseph
    *Letters addressed to the Philosophers and Politicians of France
      on the subject of Religion
          London, 1793

(507)   B36
[PUECKLER-MUSKAU (Pückler-Muskau), Hermann, *Prince*]
    Tour in England, Ireland, and France [1826-1829]. With remarks
      on the manners and customs of the inhabitants . . . in a series
      of letters by a German Prince
          Philadelphia, 1833

(508)   B57, B58
PULTENEY, Richard
    A General View of the Writings of Linnæus: (2nd edition, with
      additions and memoirs of the author by William George
      Maton, including a translation of Linnæus' Diary)
          London, 1805

Q

(509)   HD28, B30, B53, B55
QUARTERLY
    The Quarterly Review
          London, 1809-1879   (148 vols.)

(510)   B51, B68
QUATREMERE DE QUINCY, Antoine Chrysostome
    An Essay on the Nature, the End, and the Means of Imitation
      in the Fine Arts (tr. J. C. Kent)
          London, 1837

R

(511) B40

RABELAIS, François
 Œuvres de Rabelais (édition variorum, with remarks by Le
  Duchat, Bernier, Le Motteux, l'abbe de Marsy, Voltaire etc.,
  and with commentary by Esmangart and Eloi Johanneau.
   Paris, 1823 (9 vols.)
     Vols. 1-2: "Gargantua et Pantagruel"

(512) B42

RALEIGH, *Sir* Walter
 The History of the World
   *London, 1666

(513) B65

RANDOLPH, Herbert *editor*
 Life of General Sir Robert Wilson from autobiographical memoirs,
  journals, etc. (ed. by his nephew)
   London, 1862 (2 vols.)

(514) B54

RAUMER, Friedrich Ludwig Georg von
 ? England in 1835 (tr. Sarah Austen and H. Evans Lloyd)
   London, 1836 (3 vols.)
   Philadelphia, 1836 (3 vols.)
 ? England in 1841 (tr. H. Evans Lloyd)
   London, 1842 (2 vols.)

(515) B32

RAYNAL, Guillaume Thomas François *abbé*
 A Philosophical and Political history of the Settlements and
  trade of the Europeans in the East and West Indies (tr. J. O.
  Justamond, F.R.S.)
   London, 1783 (8 vols.)

(516) B70

READE, Charles
 The Cloister and the Hearth; or, Maid, Wife and Widow
   New York, 1861

(517) B30

REES, Abraham
 Cyclopædia [1st American edition]
   Philadelphia, [1810-1824] (41 vols. with 5 vols. of plates)

(518) B63, B69

RENAN, Ernest
 Essais de Morale et de Critique
   Paris, 1860 (2ᵉ édition)

(519) B64

RENAN, Ernest
 The Life of Jesus (tr. C. E. Wilbour)
   New York, 1864

(520) B64

RENAN, Ernest
 Vie de Jésus
   Paris, 1863

(521) B34, B35

RETROSPECTIVE
 The Retrospective Review and Historical and Antiquarian Maga-
  zine
   London, 1820-1827 (15 vols.)

(522)   B54
RETZ, Jean François Paul de Gondi, *cardinal* de
     Memoirs of the Cardinal de Retz
         Philadelphia, 1817   (3 vols.)

(523)   B54, B55, B58, B60, B64, B67, B68, B70
REVUE
     Revue des deux Mondes
         Paris, 1831-1879   (234 vols.)

(524)   B57
RICHTER, Jean Paul Friedrich
     Jean Paul's Sämmtliche Werke
         Berlin, 1840-1842   (33 vols.)
                Vol. 27: "Museum"; "Ueber die deutschen Doppel-
                   wörter"
                Vol. 28: "Der Komet"; "Briefe an F. H. Jacobi"

(525)   B67
RITTER, Karl
     The Comparative Geography of Palestine and the Sinaitic
     Peninsula (tr. William L. Gage)
         New York, 1866   (2 vols.)

(525a)   B32
ROBERTSON, William
     The History of America
         London, 1800   (9th ed., 4 vols.)

(526)   H23
ROBERTSON, William
     The History of Scotland
         *Philadelphia, 1811   (1st American edition, 2 vols.)

(527)   B60
ROGERS, Samuel
     Recollections
         Boston, 1859

(528)   B60
ROGERS, Samuel
     Recollections of the Table-Talk of Samuel Rogers; to which is
     added Porsoniana
         New York, 1856

(529)   B65, B69
ROLAND
     La Chanson de Roland: Poëme de Theroulde. (Texte critique,
     with translation, introd., and notes by François Génin)
         Paris, 1850

(530)   B54
ROMILLY, *Sir* Samuel
     Memoirs of the Life of Sir Samuel Romilly, written by himself
     (with a selection from his correspondence), ed. by his sons.
         London, 1840   (3 vols.)   (2nd edition)

(531)   B61
ROPER, William
     The Life of Sir Thomas More   (ed. Samuel Weller Singer)
         Chiswick, 1822

(532)   B57
ROSA, Salvator
     *Serie di 85 Disegni, incisi da C. Antonini
         Roma, 1780

(533)   B36

ROSS, *Sir* John
      Narrative of a Second Voyage in search of a North-west Passage
          (1829-1833), including reports of Capt. J. C. Ross and the
          discovery of the northern magnetic pole
                Philadelphia, 1835
                London, 1835

(534)   B32, B34

ROYAL SOCIETY OF LONDON
      Philosophical Transactions for the years 1813, 1816, 1822
                London, 1813, 1816, 1822   (3 vols.)

(535)   B66

RUSKIN, John
      The Ethics of the Dust: ten lectures to little housewives on the
          elements of crystallisation
                London, 1866

(536)   B59

RUSKIN, John
      Modern Painters
          *New York, 1855-1860   (5 vols.)

(537)   B70

RUSKIN, John
      The Queen of the Air: being a study of the Greek myths of cloud
          and storm
                London, 1869

(538)   B51, B52

RUSKIN, John
      The Stones of Venice
                London, 1851-1853   (3 vols.)

(539)   B71

RUSKIN, John
      The Two Paths: being lectures on art and its application to
          decoration and manufacture
                London, 1859

(540)   B45

RUSSELL, Michael *bishop of Glasgow and Galloway*
      Life of Cromwell
                New York, [1838]   (2 vols.)
                      (Harper's Family Library, vols. 62-63)

(542)   B31

RUSSELL, William
      History of Modern Europe, with an account of the decline and
          fall of the Roman Empire
                London, 1786   (5 vols.)
                Philadelphia, 1800-1801   (5 vols.)
                *Philadelphia, 1815-1822   (6 vols., with continuation by
                      Charles Coote)

(543)   B63

RUSSELL, William Howard
      My Diary North and South
                Boston, 1863   (2nd American edition)

S

(544)   B62, B63
SADI (SAADI), Musli uddin
    The Gulistan or Flower Garden (tr. into prose and verse, with
        life of the author from the Atish kadar, by Edward B. East-
        wick)
            Hertford, 1852

(545)   H46, B62
SADI (SAADI), Musli uddin
    The Gulistan or Flower Garden; tr. by James Ross from the
        Persian text of Gentius, with an essay on Sadi
            London, 1823

(546)   B63
SADI (SAADI), Musli uddin
    Lustgarten; aus dem persischen übersetzt von C. H. Graf
            Jena, 1850   (2 vols.)

(547)   B64
SADI (SAADI), Musli uddin
    Rosengarten; nach dem texte und dem arabischen commentare
        Sururi's tr. and ed. K. H. Graf)
            Leipzig, 1846

(548)   H28
SAINT-EVREMOND, Charles de Marguetel de Saint-Denis de
    Works   (tr. from the French)
            London, 1700-1705   (3 vols.)

(549)   B51
ST. JOHN, James Augustus
    The History of the Manners and Customs of Ancient Greece
            London, 1842   (3 vols.)

(550)   B65, B67
SAINT-SIMON, Louis de Rouvroy, *duc* de
    Mémoires complets et authentiques
            Paris, 1829-1830   (21 vols.)

(551)   B53, B54, B56, B63, B64, B66, B67
SAINTE-BEUVE, Charles Augustin
    Causeries du Lundi
            Paris, 1851-1862   (15 vols.)

(552)   B60, B63, B64, B68
SAINTE-BEUVE, Charles Augustin
    Nouveaux Lundis
            Paris, 1863-1870   (12 vols.)

(553)   B63, B64, B68
SAINTE-BEUVE, Charles Augustin
    Portraits Contemporains
            Paris, 1852   (3 vols.)

(554)   B63, B64
SAINTE-BEUVE, Charles Augustin
    Portraits de Femmes
            Paris, 1852   (nouv. édition)

(555)   B63, B65
SAINTE-BEUVE, Charles Augustin
    Portraits Littéraires
            Paris, 1852   (nouv. édition, 2 vols.)

(556) B59
SANDERS, Daniel Hendel
 Das Volksleben der Neugriechen, aus Liedern, Sprichwörtern,
   Kunstgedichten
     Mannheim, 1844

(557) H28
SARPI, Paolo
 The Historie of the Councel of Trent, written in Italian by
   Pietro Soave Polano [pseud.] (tr. by Nathanael Brent)
     London, 1640 (3rd edition)

(558) B30
SAVAGE, John
 A Compleat History of Germany
     London, 1702
         (This is considered vol. 1 of a 2-vol. set, the second
           having the title: The Antient and Present State
           of the Empire of Germany, London, 1702.)

(559) B51, B70
SCHILLER, Johann Christoph Friedrich von
 Correspondence between Schiller and Goethe, from 1794 to 1805
   (tr. George H. Calvert)
     New York and London, 1845 (Vol. 1 all issued)

(560) B51
SCHILLER, Johann Christoph Friedrich von
 Correspondence of Schiller with Körner, comprising sketches and
   anecdotes of Goethe, the Schlegels, Wieland, and other contemporaries, with biog. sketches and notes by Leonard Simpson
     London, 1849 (3 vols.)

(561) B31
SCHILLER, Johann Christoph Friedrich von
 Wallenstein: A Drama in two parts (tr. Samuel Taylor Coleridge)
     London, 1800

(562) B45
SCHLEGEL, Friedrich von
 Lectures on the History of Literature, ancient and modern
   (tr. J. G. Lockhart)
     Edinburgh, 1818 (2 vols.)
     Philadelphia, 1818 (2 vols.)

(563) B35
SCHLEGEL, Friedrich von
 Sämmtliche Werke
     Wien, 1822 (2 vols. of a 10-vol. set)

(564) H48
SCHLEIERMACHER, Friedrich
 Schleiermacher's Introductions to the Dialogues of Plato (tr.
   from German by William Dobson)
     Cambridge and London, 1836

(565) B69
SCHWEGLER, Albert
 Handbook of the History of Philosophy (tr. and annotated by
   James H. Stirling)
     Edinburgh, 1868 (2nd edition)

(566) B34
SCORESBY, William
 An Account of the Arctic Regions, with a history and description
   of the northern whale-fishery
     Edinburgh, 1820 (2 vols.)

(567)   B31
SCOTT, John   (1639-1695)
    The Christian Life
        *London, 1694-1697   (4 vols.)

(568)   B34
SCOTT, *Sir* Walter, *bart., compiler*
    Minstrelsy of the Scottish Border
        Edinburgh, 1810   (4th ed., 3 vols.)

(569)   B30
SELDEN, John
    Table Talk [1689]
        Edinburgh, 1819

(570)   H48, H68
SEWELL, William
    An Introduction to the Dialogues of Plato
        London, 1841

(571)   B69
SHAIRP, John Campbell
    Studies in Poetry and Philosophy
        Edinburgh, 1868
    (Contents: Wm. Wordsworth, S. T. Coleridre, John Keble etc.)

(572)   H17, H23
SHAKESPEARE, William
    Works   (I cannot identify the editions.)

(573)   H35, B35, B38
SHAKESPEARE, William
    The Plays and Poems of William Shakespeare (ed. Edmond
        Malone [and James Boswell])
            London, 1821   (21 vols.)
                (Vols. 1-3: "Prolegomena")

(574)   B45
SHELLEY, Percy Bysshe
    Essays, Letters from Abroad, Translations and Fragments
        (ed. Mrs. [Mary Wollstonecraft (Godwin)] Shelley)
            London, 1840   (2 vols.)
    (Contains: "A Defence of Poetry"
                "Essay on Literature, Arts, and Manners of
                    Athenians"
                "The Banquet" (translated from Plato)
                "On Love"; "On Life"; "On a Future State"
                "Ion; or, Of the Iliad" (tr. from Plato)
                "Fragments of the Republic of Plato" etc. etc.)

(575)   B52
SHERIDAN, Richard Brinsley
    The Works of the Late Rt. Hon. Richard Brinsley Sheridan
        London, 1821   (2 vols.)

(576)   H35, B54
SIDNEY, *Sir* Philip
    Miscellaneous Works; with a Life of the author and notes by
        William Gray
            Oxford, 1829

(577)   B42
SIDNEY, *Sir* Philip
    The Works of the Hon. Sir Philip Sidney, Knight
        London, 1725   (14th ed., 3 vols.)

(578)   B68, B72
SKENE, William Forbes
    The Four Ancient Books of Wales, containing the Cymric poems
        attributed to the bards of the Sixth Century
                Edinburgh, 1868   (2 vols.)
                    (Vol. 1 contains the English translation)

(579)   B66
SMALL, George
    A Handbook of Sanskrit Literature: with appendices descriptive
        of the mythology, castes, and religious sects of the Hindus
            London, 1866

(580)   B57
SMILES, Samuel
    The Life of George Stephenson, railway engineer
            London, 1857

(581)   H28
SMITH, *Sir* James Edward
    An Introduction to Physiological and Systematical Botany
        (with notes by Jacob Bigelow)
            Boston, 1814

(582)   B31
SMITH, John, *rector of St. Mary's Colchester*
    Christian Religion's Appeal from the Groundless Prejudices of
        the Sceptick, to the bar of Common Reason
            London, 1675   (2 vols. bound in 1. Emerson apparently
                used the volumes when they were separate.)

(583)   B60, B64
SNORRI STURLUSON (*or* Snorro Sturleson)
    The Heimskringla; or, Chronicle of the Kings of Norway (tr.
        Samuel Laing)
            London, 1844   (3 vols.)

(584)   B37
SOPHOCLES
    Tragedies (translated by R. Potter)
            London, 1820   (new edition)

(585)   B36
SOPHOCLES
    *Tragœdiæ Septem ad optimorum exemplarium fidem emendatæ
        cum versione et notis ex editione R. F. P. Brunck
            Argentorati, 1786-1789   (4 vols.)

(586)   H23
SOUTH, Robert
    Sermons
            London, 1724-1727   (6 vols.)
            London, 1734-1744   (11 vols.)

(587)   B31, B36, B68
SOUTHEY, Robert
    The Book of the Church
            London, 1825   (2 vols.)

(588)   B38
SOUTHEY, Robert
    The Doctor &c.
            London, 1834-1847   (7 vols.)

(589)   B32
SOUTHEY, Robert
    Essays, moral and political
            London, 1832   (2 vols.)

(590)   B35
SOUTHEY, Robert
> History of the Peninsula War
> > London, 1828-1837   (6 vols.)

(591)   B53
SOUTHEY, Robert
> The Life and Correspondence of Robert Southey (ed. by his son,
> Charles Cuthbert Southey)
> > London, 1849-1850   (2nd ed., 6 vols.)

(592)   B60, B61
SOUTHEY, Robert
> Southey's Common-Place Book (the first three series, ed. by
> John Wood Warter)
> > London, 1849-1850   (3 vols.)

(593)   B32
SOUTHEY, Thomas
> Chronological History of the West Indies
> > London, 1827   (3 vols.)

(594)   B30, B38
SPENCE, Joseph
> Anecdotes, Observations, and Characters of books and men, col-
> lected from the conversation of Mr. Pope and other eminent
> persons of his time. (With notes and life by Samuel Weller
> Singer)
> > London, 1820

(595)   H35
SPENSER, Edmund
> The Poetical Works of Edmund Spenser (from the text of John
> Upton etc.)
> > London, 1787-1788   (8 vols.)
> The Works of Edmund Spenser (with notes and life by Henry
> John Todd)
> > London, 1805   (8 vols.)

(596)   B40
SPENSER, Edmund
> Poetical Works (ed. with notes by G. S. Hillard)
> > Boston, 1839 (5 vols.)
> > > Vol. 5: "Miscellaneous Poems"

(597)   B39
STAEL-HOLSTEIN, Anne Louise Germaine (Necker), *baronne de*
> Corinna; or, Italy
> > Boston, 1808   (2 vols.)

(598)   B34, B45
STAEL-HOLSTEIN, Anne Louise Germaine (Necker), *baronne de*
> Œuvres complètes
> > Paris, 1820-1821   (17 vols.)
> > > Vol. 6-7: "Delphine"; vol. 8: "Corinne"
> > > Vol. 15: "Dix Années d'Exil"

(599)   B68
STAHR, Adolf
> Weimar und Jena; ein Tagebuch
> > Oldenburg, 1852   (2 vols.)

(600)   B64, B67
STANHOPE, Philip Dormer *4th earl of Chesterfield*
    ? Letters written . . . to his Son, Philip Stanhope
        Boston, 1869   (2 vols.)
    ? Letters (ed. with notes by Lord Mahon [Philip Henry Stan-
    hope]
        London, 1845-1853   (5 vols.)
(601)   B34
STANLEY, Thomas
    The History of Philosophy
        London, 1701   (3rd edition)
(602)   B70
STEFFENS, Henrich
    The Story of My Career as Student at Freiberg and Jena, and
    as Professor at Halle, Breslau, and Berlin; with reminiscences
    of Goethe, Schiller, Schelling [and others]
    (tr. by William Leonhard Gage)
        Boston, 1863
(603)   H26
STEWART, Dugald
    Elements of the Philosophy of the Human Mind
        (Edition uncertain)
(604)   B37
STRUTT, Joseph
    The Chronicle of England
        London, 1777[-1778]   (2 vols.)
(605)   B37
STRUTT, Joseph
    Queenhoo Hall, a romance; and Ancient Times, a drama
    (ed. by Sir Walter Scott)
        Edinburgh, 1808   (4 vols.)
(606)   H23
SULLIVAN, James *governor*
    The History of the District of Maine
        Boston, 1795
(607)   H23
SULLY, Maximilien de Béthune, *duc* de
    Memoirs. Containing the history of the reign of [Henry IV]
    (tr. from the French by Charlotte Lennox)
        London, 1757   (5 vols.)
        London, 1761   (3 vols.)
    (See item 608)
(608)   B32
SULLY, Maximilien de Béthune, *duc* de
    The Memoirs of the Duke of Sully, Prime-Minister to Henry the
    Great (tr. from the French by Charlotte Lennox)
        Philadelphia, 1817 (5 vols.)
    (See item 607)
(609)   B66
SWINBURNE, Algernon Charles
    Atalanta in Calydon; a Tragedy
        London, 1865

T

(610)   B66
TAINE, Hippolyte Adolphe
    Histoire de la Littérature anglaise
        Paris, 1863-1864   (4 vols.)

(611)   B69
TAINE, Hippolyte Adolphe
    The Ideal in Art (tr. John Durand)
        New York, 1869

(612)   B72
TAINE, Hippolyte Adolphe
    Notes sur Paris: Vie et opinions de M. Frédéric-Thomas
        Graindorge
        Paris, 1867

(613)   B68
TAINE, Hippolyte Adolphe
    Nouveaux Essais de Critique et d'histoire
        Paris, 1865

(614)   B58
TAUTPHŒUS, Jemima (Montgomery) *freifrau* von
    Quits: a Novel
        Philadelphia, 1857   (2 vols. in 1)

(615)   B71
TAYLOR, *Sir* Henry
    Edwin the Fair. An Historical Drama
        London, 1842

(616)   HD27, HD28, HD29, B31, B32
TAYLOR, Jeremy, *bp. of Down, Connor and Dromore*
    The Whole Works (with life etc. by Reginald Heber)
        London, 1822   (15 vols.)

(617)   B52
TAYLOR, William Cooke
    Life and Times of Sir Robert Peel
        London, [1846-1851]   (4 vols.)

(618)   B32
TEMMINCK, Coenraad Jacob
    Manuel d'Ornithologie, ou Tableau systématique des oiseaux qui
        se trouvent en Europe
        Paris, 1820-1835   (2nd ed.)   (Athenæum has only 3 out
            of a 4-volume set.)

(619)   B62
THACKERAY, William Makepeace
    The Four Georges: Sketches of manners, morals, court and town
        life
        New York, 1860

(620)   B53
THIERRY, Augustin
    History of the Conquest of England by the Normans
        London, 1841

(621)   B67
THIERS, Adolphe
    Histoire du Consulat et de l'Empire
        Paris, 1845-1862   (20 vols.)

(622)   B69
THOLUCK, August
    Blüthensämmlnng aus der morgenländischen Mystik
        Berlin, 1825

(623)   B67
THOMPSON, D'Arcy Wentworth
    Day Dreams of a Schoolmaster
        Edinburgh, 1864   (2nd ed.)

(624)   B69
THOMPSON, D'Arcy Wentworth
    Sales Attici; or the Maxims witty and wise of Athenian
    tragic drama
            Edinburgh, 1867

(625)   B62
THORNBURY, George Walter
    The Life of Joseph Mallord William Turner
            London, 1862   (2 vols.)

(626)   H24
TILLOTSON, John *archbishop of Canterbury*
    Works (with his life by Thomas Birch)
            *London, 1752   (3 vols.)

(627)   B60
TOEPFER (Töpfer), Rodolphe
    Premiers Voyages en Zigzag, ou Excursions d'un Pensionnat en
    Vacances dans les Cantons Suisses et sur le Revers Italien des
    Alpes
            Paris, 1855   (4° édition)

(628)   B71
TOTTEL, Richard *editor*
    Tottel's Miscellany: Songes and Sonettes by Henry Howard Earl
    of Surrey, Sir Thomas Wyatt, Nicholas Grimald . . . 1557 (ed.
    Edward Arber
            London, 1870   (Arber's English Reprints, vol. 11)

(629)   B32
TRACTS bearing the shelf number "B 781" contained the following:

        (630)
    Jenkinson, Charles
            A Discourse on the Conduct of the Government of Great
            Britain in respect to Neutral Nations
                    London, 1801

        (631)
    Bowles, John
            Reflections at the Conclusion of the War
                    London, 1801

        (632)
    Vindication
            A Vindication of the Convention lately concluded between
            Great Britain and Russia. In six letters . . .
                    London, 1801

        (633)
    Fox, Charles James
            The Speech of the Hon. Charles James Fox, on the
            motion for an enquiry into the State of the Nation
            (Mar. 25, 1801)
                    London, 1801

        (634)
    Boyd, Walter
            A Letter to the Rt. Hon. William Pitt, on the Influence
            of the Stoppage of Issues in Specie at the Bank of
            England
                    London, 1801

(635)
Mackintosh, James
A Discourse on the Study of the Law of Nature and Nations; introductory to a course of lectures on that Science
London, 1800 (3rd edition)

(636)
Fox, Charles James
The Speech (at length) of the Hon. C. J. Fox, against the Address to his Majesty, approving of the Refusal to enter into a negotiation for peace with the French Republic
London, 1800

(637)   B56
TRENCH, Richard Chenevix, *abp. of Dublin*
Calderon, his life and genius, with specimens of his plays
New York, 1856

(638)   B55
TRENCH, Richard Chenevix, *abp. of Dublin*
On the Lessons in Proverbs (From the 2nd London ed., revised and enlarged)
New York, 1853

(639)   B35, B37
TURNER, Sharon
History of the Anglo-Saxons
London, 1807 (2nd ed., 2 vols.)

(640)   B63
TYNDALL, John
Heat; a mode of motion
London, 1863

(641)   B68
TYNDALL, John
Sound: a course of eight lectures
London, 1867

(642)   B42
TYTLER, Patrick Fraser
Life of Sir Walter Raleigh (including a view of the most important transactions in the reigns of Elizabeth and James I, with a vindication of his character from the attacks of Hume etc.
Edinburgh, 1833 (Edinburgh Cabinet Library, vol. 11)

U

(643)   B72
UNITED STATES, *Department of Agriculture*
Report of the Commissioner of Agriculture for the Year 1865
Washington, 1866

(644)   H31
UNITED STATES, *State Papers*
State Papers of the United States (1801-1806)
(Edition uncertain)

(645)   H46
UPHAM, Edward
The History and Doctrine of Budhism [sic], with notices of the demon worship and planetary incantations of Ceylon
London, 1829

V

(646)   B70
VARNHAGEN VON ENSE, Karl August Ludwig Philipp
    Blätter aus der preussischen Geschichte
        Leipzig, 1868-1869   (5 vols.)

(647)   B63, B64
VARNHAGEN VON ENSE, Karl August Ludwig Philipp
    Denkwürdigkeiten und vermischte Schriften
        Leipzig, 1843-1859   (2ᵉ Aufl., 9 vols.)

(648)   B63, B64, B70, B71
VARNHAGEN VON ENSE, Karl August Ludwig Philipp
    Tagebücher von Varnhagen von Ense (hrsg. Ludmilla Assing)
        Leipzig, 1861-1870   (14 vols.)

(649)   H34, H55
VASARI, Giorgio
    Vite de' Piu' Eccellenti Pittori, Scultori, e Architetti
        Milano, 1807-1811   (16 vols.)

(650)   B55, B60, B66
VEDAS
    Rig-veda-sanhitá. A collection of ancient Hindu hymns (tr. from
    the original Sanskrit by Horace Hayman Wilson)
        London, 1850-1866   (4 vols.)

(651)   B71, B72
VICTORIA, *queen of Great Britain, sponsor*
    The Early Years of His Royal Highness the Prince Consort
    (compiled by Charles Grey)
        London, 1867
        New York, 1867

(652)   B67
VIGNY, Alfred, *comte* de
    Cinq-Mars: or, a conspiracy under Louis XIII: An historical
    romance. (tr. from the 9th Paris ed. by William Hazlitt)
        *London, 1847
        (There are several French editions which Emerson might
           have used.)

(653)   B45
VILLEMAREST, Charles Maxime Catherinet de
    Life of Prince Talleyrand
        London, 1834-1836   (4 vols.)

(654)   B65
VIOLLET-LE-DUC, Eugène Emmanuel
    Entretiens sur l'Architecture
        Paris, 1863   (Tome 1 only)

(655)   B68
VITRUVIUS POLLIO, Marcus
    The Architecture of Marcus Vitruvius Pollio (tr. from the Latin
    by Joseph Gwilt; a new edition revised)
        London, 1860
        (This comprises vols. 128-129 of John Weale's Series of
           Rudimentary Works in 152 vols., London, 1850-1860)

(656)   H28
VOLNEY, Constantin François Chassebœuf, *comte* de
    The Ruins: or, A survey of the revolutions of empires
        *London, 1804   (12th edition)
        (Some editions have Volney's *The Law of Nature* at-
           tached.)

(657)   H26

VOLTAIRE, François Marie Arouet de
     The General History and State of Europe, from the time of
        Charlemain to Charles V. (From the French)
           London, 1754-1757   (3 vols.)

(658)   H50

VOLTAIRE, François Marie Arouet de
     Œuvres Complètes de Voltaire
        [Kehl], 1785-1789   (70 vols.)
           Vols. 20-21: "Siècle de Louis XIV"

(659)   B52, B68

VOLTAIRE, François Marie Arouet de
     Œuvres Complètes de Voltaire (ed. Pierre Beaumarchais, Mar-
        quis de Condorcet and Jacques Decroix)
        [Kehl], 1785-1789   (92 vols.)
           Vol. 56: "Zadig etc."
           Vol. 57: "L'Ingènu, histoire veritable etc."
           Vol. 61: "Panegyric de Louis XV. etc."

W

(660)   B55

WAAGEN, Gustav Friedrich
     Treasures of Art in Great Britain
           London, 1854   (3 vols.)

(661)   B42

WAAGEN, Gustav Friedrich
     Works of Art and Artists in England (tr. H. E. Lloyd)
           London, 1838   (3 vols.)

(662)   B30

WAKEFIELD, Gilbert
     Correspondence of the late Gilbert Wakefield with Rt. Hon.
        Charles James Fox (1796-1801), chiefly on subjects of classi-
        cal literature
           London, 1813

(663)   HD28

WARBURTON, William, *bishop of Gloucester*
     Works (new ed., with account of his life etc. by Richard Hurd)
           London, 1811   (12 vols.)

(664)   H47

WARD, William
     Account of the writings, religion, and manners of the Hindoos,
        including translations of their principal works
           Serampore, 1811   (4 vols.)

(665)   B72

WARE, William
     Zenobia: or, The Fall of Palmyra: An historical romance
           New York, 1839   (2 vols.)

(666)   B70

WARING, Anna Letitia
     Hymns and Meditations (with introd. by F. D. Huntington.
        From 8th London edn.)
           Boston, 1863

(667)   B61
WARNER, Anna Bartlett (*pseud.*: Amy Lothrop)
      Dollars and Cents [A Novel]
           New York, 1852   (2 vols.)

(668)   B35
WARTON, Thomas
      The History of English Poetry (New ed. by Richard Price)
           London, 1824   (4 vols.)

(669)   B61
WATSON, John Selby
      The Life of Richard Porson
           London, 1861

(670)   B63
WEALE, John
      Quarterly Papers on Architecture
           London, 1844-1845   (4 vols.)

(671)   B61
WELCKER, Friedrich Gottlieb
      Alte Denkmäler erklärt
           Göttingen, 1849-1864   (5 vols. besides plates)

(672)   B34
WELLS, William Charles
      An Essay on Dew and several appearances connected with it
           London, 1815   (2nd edition)

(673)   B32, B60
WESTMINSTER
      Westminster Review
           London, 1824-1851   (56 vols.)

(674)   B69
WEZEL, Johann Karl
      Belphegor, oder Die wahrscheinlichste Geschichte unter der Sonne
           Leipzig, 1776   (2 vols.)

(675)   B67
WHEELER, James Talboys
      The History of India from the Earliest Ages
           London, 1867-1876   (4 vols.)

(676)   B32, B39
WHITE, Gilbert
      The Natural History and Antiquities of Selborne
           London, 1825   (new ed., 2 vols.)

(677)   B66
WHITE, Richard Grant *compiler and editor*
      Poetry lyrical, narrative, and satirical of the Civil War
           New York, 1866

(678)   B67
WHITE, William *of Hampstead, England*
      Emanuel Swedenborg: his life and writings
           London, 1867   (2 vols.)

(679)   B61
WHITEHEAD, Charles Edward
      Wild Sports in the South, or, The camp-fires of the Everglades
           New York, 1860

(680)   B34, B35, B37, B45, B54, B57, B69
WIELAND, Christoph Martin
    Sämmtliche Werke (hrsg. J. G. Gruber)
        Leipzig, 1824-1826   (49 vols. out of a 53-vol. set)

(681)   B66
WILKINSON, *Sir* John Gardner
    The Egyptians in the time of the Pharaohs (also an introd. to
    the study of Egyptian hieroglyphs, by Samuel Birch)
        London, 1857

(682)   B68
WILKINSON, *Sir* John Gardner
    ?Manners and Customs of the Ancient Egyptians
        London, 1842-1837   (3 vols.: vol. 1 of 2nd ed.: others 1st.)
    ?A Second Series of the Manners and Customers of the Ancient
    Egyptians
        London, 1841   (2 vols.)

(683)   B58
WILKINSON, *Sir* John Gardner
    Modern Egypt and Thebes
        London, 1843   (2 vols.)

(684)   B37
WILSON, Alexander; *and* Charles Lucien Bonaparte
    American Ornithology; or, The natural history of the birds of
    the United States (ed. Robert Jameson)
        Edinburgh, 1831   (4 vols.)
        (Constable's Miscellany, vols. 68-71)

(685)   B61
WILSON, *Sir* Robert Thomas
    Private Diary of Travels, personal services, and public events,
    during mission and employment with the European armies in
    the campaigns of 1812, 1813, 1814 (ed. Herbert Randolph)
        London, 1861   (2 vols.)

(686)   B31
WILSON, Walter
    Memoirs of the Life and Times of Daniel De Foe; containing a
    review of his writings, and his opinions upon a variety of im-
    portant matters, civil and ecclesiastical
        London, 1830   (3 vols.)

(687)   B61
WINTHROP, John *governor of Massachusetts*
    The History of New England from 1630 to 1649 (with notes by
    James Savage)
        Boston, 1825-1826   (2 vols.)
        Boston, 1853   (2 vols.)

(688)   B72
WITTE, Karl
    Dante-Forschungen, altes und neues
        Berlin, 1869

(689)   H25
WOLLASTON, William
    The Religion of Nature Delineated
        *London, 1738   (6th edition)

(690)   B68
WORDSWORTH, Christopher *bishop of Lincoln*
    Athens and Attica: Journal of a Residence there.
        London, 1855   (3rd edition revised)

(691)   HD28, HD29, B68, B69, B72
WORDSWORTH, William
    Poetical Works
        Boston, 1824   (4 vols.)

(692)   H28
WOTTON, *Sir* Henry
    *Reliquiae Wottonianæ
        London, 1672   (3rd edition)

(693)   B53
WRAXALL, *Sir* Nathaniel William *bart.*
    Historical Memoirs of My Own Time
        London, 1815   (2 vols.)

(694)   B52, B53
WRAXALL, *Sir* Nathaniel William *bart.*
    Posthumous Memoirs of his Own Time
        London, 1836   (3 vols.)

Y

(695)   B60
*YOUATT, William
    The Horse: with a treatise on draught; and a copious index
        London, 1831   (Library of Useful Knowledge)

SUPPLEMENTARY

OR

CROSS - REFERENCE INDEX
TO THE PRECEDING BIBLIOGRAPHY

Emphasizing Subjects, Places, Names of Translators and Editors,
Pseudonyms and Catchwords (Exclusive of All Elements
Constituting the Alphabetical System of the
Foregoing Pages)

CROSS-REFERENCE INDEX*

A

B

*All numbers refer to the items in the foregoing bibliography.

SOME
UNEDITED EMERSON
LETTERS

I

Of the two surviving Emerson letters mentioning Mr. Gugliel-
mo Gajani, author of *The Roman Exile,* Professor Rusk was able
to edit only one.[1] He merely referred to the second,[2] setting
forth a few details gathered from an inaccurate bookseller's
announcement. This manuscript, which was apparently written
to Charles Thomas Jackson, Emerson's brother-in-law, has re-
cently come into my possession, and I print it here entire:

Concord 6 May 1856

My dear brother,

     I enclose $11.00 whereof $10. were
kindly lent me by you on Friday last, & 1.00 was
received by me today for one of Mr. Gajani's books;
& will you please give it to Susan for him.

Yours affectionately,

R. W. Emerson.

II

Another unpublished letter appears in a manuscript volume of
records belonging to the Harvard Theological School in Cambridge and is interesting because it indicates the circumstances
under which Emerson consented to deliver his Divinity School
Address. Unfortunately it is only a copy of the original, now

---

[1]See Ralph L. Rusk, *The Letters of Ralph Waldo Emerson,* N. Y., 1939,
V, pp. 13-14.
 [2]*Ibid.,* V, 21.

probably lost, but as a part of the Divinity School archives deserves to be better known:*

Concord 27 March 1838

Gentlemen,

Will you signify to the members of the Senior Class in the Divinity College, that it will give me pleasure to comply with their request, and to speak to them on Sunday evening 15 July next, on the occasion of their entering upon the active Christian Ministry.

In the good hope of our calling, I am

Your friend and servant,

R. W. Emerson

Messrs. Geo. F. Simmons ⎤
       M. G. O. Blake   ⎬ Committee
       W. D. Wilson   ⎦

---

*See *The Records of the Theological School*, a manuscript volume numbered 900.11, folio 96, in the Andover-Harvard Theological Library. On folio 99, under date of July 15, the following note appears: "This evening Rev. R. W. Emerson preached a sermon to the Senior Class. The Chapel was very much crowded, and the discourse listened to with profound attention."

EMERSON'S CONTEMPORARIES
(1827———1850)

Whose Book Borrowings Are Inscribed
In the Charging Records of the
BOSTON ATHENÆUM

(A)   Charging Records, Volume I   (1827-1834)

(B)   Charging Records, Volume II   (1835-1843)

(C)   Charging Records, Volume III   (1844-1849)

(D)   Charging Records, Volume IV   (1849-1850)

(Later volumes are not analyzed here.)

A

Abbot, Samuel L. *M.D.*	(BCD)
Abbott, Rev. Jacob	(BCD)
Adams, Mrs. A. B.	(D)
Adams, Caleb Benjamin	(A)
Adams, Charles Francis	(ABCD)
Adams, Charles Frederick	(C)
Adams, Francis M.	(CD)
Adams, Miss Hannah	(A)
Adams, John C.	(C)
Adams, Zabdiel B. *M.D.*	(ABCD)
Aiken, Rev. Silas	(B)
Alcott, A. Bronson	(CD)
Alexander, Andrew *M.D.*	(CD)
Alger, Cyrus	(ABC)
Alger, Francis	(BCD)
Allen, James	(A)
Allen, Robert B.	(A)
Amory, Charles	(CD)
Amory, Jonathan	(A)
Amory, Thomas C. Jr.	(CD)
Amory, William	(CD)
Anderson, Rev. Rufus	(AB)
Andrews, Caleb	(AB)
Andrews, James	(AB)
Andrews, William T.	(ABCD)
Appleton, Eben	(A)
Appleton, F. H.	(C)
Appleton, Nathan	(ABCD)
Appleton, Samuel	(ACD)
Appleton, William	(ABCD)
Apthorp, John T.	(A)
Armstrong, Samuel T.	(A)
Arvine, Rev. K. (of West Boylston)	(D)
Atkinson, Edward	(CD)
Atkinson, William P.	(BCD)
Atwood, Charles	(BCD)
Austin, Henry D.	(CD)
Austin, James T.	(AB)
Austin, Samuel	(BCD)
Aylwin, William C.	(C)

B

Bacon, Daniel C.	(C)
Baker, A. R.	(C)
Balch, Joseph	(CD)
Ball, Dr. Stephen	(D)
Bancroft, George	(AB)
Bangs, George P.	(D)
Bangs, Edward	(C)
Barnard, Charles	(ABCD)
Barnes, Isaac O.	(D)
Bartlett, Thomas	(AB)
Barrell, Samuel B.	(B)
Barrett, Rev. Samuel	(ABC)

Bartlett, Sidney	(CD)
Bartol, Rev. Cyrus A.	(BCD)
Bass, Seth	(AD)
Bassett, Francis	(BD)
Bates, George *M.D.*	(ABCD)
Beck, Charles	(CD)
Becker, Mrs.	(D)
Beecher, Edward	(C)
Belknap, Andrew E.	(CD)
Belknap, John	(ABCD)
Bell, Joseph	(BCD)
Bemis, Samuel A.	(A)
Bethune, John M.	(BCD)
Bigelow, E. B.	(D)
Bigelow, Henry J. *M.D.*	(D)
Bigelow, Horatio	(D)
Bigelow, Jacob *M.D.*	(ABCD)
Bigelow, John P.	(A)
Binney, Mrs. A.	(D)
Binney, Amos	(ABC)
Bird, John A.	(CD)
Blagden, Rev. George W.	(ABCD)
Blake, Edward	(B)
Blake, James H.	(A)
Blake, Joshua	(B)
Blake, Samuel P.	(ABCD)
Blake, William	(CD)
Blanchard, Edward	(CD)
Blanchard, John A.	(CD)
Bliss, William D.	(D)
Bogen, Rev. Frederic W.	(D)
Bokum, Hermann	(B)
Bond, George	(A)
Booth, C. H.	(C)
Boott, Francis	(ABC)
Boott, John William	(AB)
Boott, Kirk	(AB)
Borland, J. Nelson	(D)
Borland, John	(A)
Bowditch, Henry J. *M.D.*	(BCD)
Bowditch, J. Ingersoll	(BCD)
Bowditch, Nathaniel *LL.D.*	(AB)
Bowditch, Nathaniel Ingersol	(BCD)
Bowdoin, James	(A)
Bowen, Francis	(BCD)
Boyden, Uriah A.	(BCD)
Bradbury, Charles	(AB)
Bradford, Thomas G.	(B)
Bradlee, Edward C.	(D)
Bradlee, Frederick W.	(D)
Bradlee, James B.	(CD)
Bradlee, Joseph P.	(A)
Bradlee, Josiah	(ABC)
Bradlee, Nathaniel J.	(D)
Bradlee, William C.	(D)
Brewer, Gardner	(CD)
Brewer, Thomas M.	(D)

Bridge, Samuel J. (A)
Briggs, William A. *M.D.* (B)
Brigham, Elijah D. (D)
Brimmer, George W. (AB)
Brimmer, Hon. Martin (ABCD)
Brooks, Edward (ABC)
Brooks, Francis A. (D)
Brooks, Francis B. (D)
Brooks, Gorham (ABCD)
Brooks, Peter C. (ABD)
Brooks, Peter C. Jr. (C)
Brooks, William G. (B)
Brooks, William H. (CD)
Brown, James (C)
Brown, Rev. John (A)
Bryant, John (ABC)
Buckingham, Joseph T. (D)
Bullard, William S. (BCD)
Bumstead, John (AB)
Burley, Miss Susan (BCD)
Burroughs, Charles (A)
Burroughs, George (ABC)
Bussey, Benjamin (A)
Butler, Rev. Clement M. (C)

C

Cabot, John H. (A)
Cabot, Samuel (BCD)
Cabot, Samuel Jr. *M.D.* (BCD)
Cabot, Thomas H. (A)
Capen, Nahum (AB)
Carrire, Jules J. (D)
Carter, James G. (A)
Cary, Miss Ann M. (D)
Cary, Thomas G. (ABCD)
Cazenove, Charles (A)
Chace, Caleb (D)
Chadwick, Ebenezer (CD)
Chandler, Abiel (A)
Chandler, Gardiner L. (ABCD)
Channing, Walter *M.D.* (AB)
Channing, Rev. Wm. E.
   D.D. (AB)
Channing, William F. (D)
Chapman, George (A)
Chapman, Jonathan (BC)
Chapman, Mrs. M. W. (CD)
Chapman, O. G. (D)
Chase, Theodore (CD)
Chase, William M. (D)
Child, Mrs. D. L. (A)
Child, David W. (A)
Choate, Hon. Rufus (BCD)
Clapp, Elisha (A)
Clark, B. C. (D)
Clark, Edward (A)
Clarke, Rev. Jas. Freeman (BCD)

Clarke, John (A)
Clinch, Rev. Joseph H. (CD)
Coale, W. C. *M.D.* (C)
Cobb, Fred A. (A)
Cobb, Richard (AB)
Codman, Charles R. (A)
Codman, Henry (ABCD)
Codman, John (A)
Coffin, George W. (CD)
Coffin, John G. (A)
Coffin, Thomas M. (CD)
Coit, Daniel T. *M.D.* (A)
Coit, Thomas W. (A)
Colburn, Warren (A)
Cole, Doctor (B)
Coleman, Henry (A)
Colman, Rev. Henry (B)
Cooke, Josiah P. (BCD)
Coolidge, John T. (D)
Coolidge, Joseph (A)
Coolidge, Joseph Jr. (A)
Coolidge, Samuel F. (A)
Cordis, Thomas (ACD)
Cotting, B. E. *M.D.* (BC)
Courties, Ambrose S. (A)
Crowninshield, B. W. (C)
Cruft, Edward (ABCD)
Cunningham, C. Loring (D)
Curtis, Benjamin R. (BCD)
Curtis, Caleb (CD)
Curtis, Charles P. (ABCD)
Curtis, Nathaniel Jr. (B)
Curtis, Thomas B. (BCD)
Cushing, Hon. Caleb (AB)
Cushing, Luther S. (CD)
Cushing, Thomas P. (CD)
Cutler, Pliney **(A)**

D

Dana, Edward (A)
Dana, Richard H. (D)
Dana, Samuel L. (A)
Danforth, Bowers (ABCD)
Darling, Benjamin (A)
Darrah, Robert K. (CD)
Davis, Edward G. (A)
Davis, Francis (C)
Davis, Isaac P. (ABC)
Davis, Mrs. J. W. (C)
Davis, J. P. (B)
Davis, Hon. John (AB)
Davis, John B. (A)
Davis, Joshua (A)
Davis, Thomas (AB)
Dearborn, H. A. S. (A)
Degrand, P. P. F. (B)
Derby, Richard C. (A)
Dexter, Franklin (ABCD)

H

Hague, Rev. William	(ABC)
Hale, Enoch *M.D.*	(ABC)
Hale, Hon. Nathan	(ABCD)
Hall, James	(A)
Hall, Hon. Joseph	(ABC)
Hall, Rev. Nathaniel	(C)
Hall, Thomas B.	(CD)
Hallet, George	(A)
Hammond, Daniel	(ABCD)
Hancock, John	(ABCD)
Hancock, John Jr.	(B)
Harris, F. William	(B)
Harris, Henry	(A)
Harris, Rev. Thaddeus M. *D.D.*	(AB)
Harris, Thaddeus W. *M.D.*	(CD)
Hastings, Daniel	(AB)
Haven, Franklin	(CD)
Hawes, Prince	(C)
Hayes, Francis B.	(CD)
Hays, Hercules M.	(A)
Hayward, George *M.D.*	(ABCD)
Hayward, James	(B)
Hayward, Joshua H.	(A)
Head, Francis C.	(A)
Head, Joseph	(AB)
Head, Joseph Jr.	(A)
Healy, Mark	(CD)
Heard, John	(B)
Heard, John Jr.	(A)
Henderson, A. A. *M.D.*	(CD)
Henshaw, David	(AB)
Henshaw, Samuel	(A)
Hicks, James H.	(B)
Higginson, Francis J.	(A)
Higginson, Henry	(AB)
Higginson, James P.	(ABCD)
Higginson, Waldo	(C)
Hillard, George	(B)
Hillard, George S.	(CD)
Hines, Rev. Mr.	(B)
Hitchcock, Rev. Robert S.	(CD)
Hoar, Doctor	(A)
Hobart, Aaron	(BC)
Hobbs, Prentiss	(A)
Hoch, H. T.	(C)
Hoit, A. G.	(BCD)
Holbrook, Henry M.	(CD)
Holmes, Abiel	(AB)
Holmes, Oliver W. *M.D.*	(BCD)
Homans, J. Smith	(D)
Homer, Charles	(CD)
Homer, Joseph W.	(CD)
Hooker, Anson Jr.	(A)
Hooper, Henry N.	(A)
Hooper, Nathaniel	(D)

Hooper, Robert W. *M.D.*	(CD)
Hooper, Samuel	(ABCD)
Horton, Henry K.	(CD)
Hosmer, Z.	(B)
Hovey, Charles F.	(CD)
Howard, John C.	(A)
Howe, Dr. Estes	(C)
Howe, George	(BD)
Howe, Jabez C.	(CD)
Howe, Joseph N.	(CD)
Howe, Samuel G. *M.D.*	(ABCD)
Howes, Frederick	(B)
Howes, William B.	(D)
Hubbard, J. P.	(B)
Hubbard, John	(A)
Hubbard, Samuel	(A)
Hunt, Lieut. E. B.	(D)
Hurd, Jos. Jr.	(A)
Hurd, William	(CD)

I

Inches, Henderson	(ABCD)
Ingalls, William *M.D.*	(ABCD)
Ingersoll, James	(C)

J

Jackson, Hon. Charles	(ABCD)
Jackson, J. B. S. *M.D.*	(B)
Jackson, James *M.D.*	(ABCD)
Jackson, Mrs. Lydia	(CD)
Jackson, P. T.	(AB)
Jaques, Henry L.	(D)
Jenks, John H.	(A)
Jenks, Rev. William *D.D.*	(ABCD)
Jewett, J. H.	(C)
Jones, Miss Anna P.	(BCD)
Jones, J.	(A)
Jones, John C.	(D)
Jones, Mrs. John Coffin	(BC)
Jones, T. C.	(A)
Jones, T. K.	(A)
Joy, Mrs.	(B)
Joy, Jos. Benjamin	(A)

K

Kendall, Abel Jr.	(D)
Kent, Moody	(B)
Kettell, Samuel	(BCD)
King, Rev. T. S.	(D)
Kirk, John F.	(C)
Kirkland, Rev. J. T. *D.D., LL.D.*	(AB)
Kittredge, Joseph G.	(D)
Knowles, Seth	(A)
Kraitser, Charles	(C)
Kuhn, George H.	(CD)

L

Lamb, Thomas	(ACD)
Lamson, Rev. Alvan *D.D.*	(BCD)
Lamson, Edwin	(D)
Lamson, John	(D)
Lawrence, Hon. Abbot	(ABCD)
Lawrence, Amos	(ABC)
Lawrence, Amos A.	(BC)
Lawrence, William	(AB)
Lawrence, William R.	(BC)
Lee, Francis	(A)·
Lee, Henry	(ABCD)
Lee, Henry Jr.	(CD)
Lee, Thomas Jr.	(AB)
Lieber, Francis	(A)
Lienon, Henry	(A)
Lincoln, Benjamin	(AD)
Lippett, Rev. G. W.	(D)
Littell, E.	(C)
Little, Charles C.	(C)
Livermore, George (of Cambridge)	(BCD)
Lloyd, James	(AC)
Lodge, Giles H. *M.D.*	(BCD)
Lodge, James	(C)
Lodge, John E.	(B)
Lord, Rev. John	(CD)
Loring, Benjamin	(A)
Loring, Caleb	(A)
Loring, Charles G.	(ABCD)
Loring, Edward G.	(ABC)
Loring, Elijah	(ABC)
Loring, Mrs. Elijah	(D)
Loring, Josiah	(AB)
Lovering, J. S.	(CD)
Lowell, Charles	(A)
Lowell, Edward F.	(A)
Lowell, Francis C.	(ABCD)
Lowell, Hon. John	(AB)
Lowell, John Jr.	(A)
Lowell, John A.	(ACD)
Lowell, Miss Rebecca Amory	(BCD)
Lunt, Rev. William P. (of Quincy)	(BCD)
Lyman, George W.	(AB)
Lyman, Hon. Theodore	(BC)
Lyman, Theodore Jr.	(A)
Lyman, William	(AB)

M

Magoun, Thatcher & Son	(D)
Malcolm, Howard	(A)
Mansfield, Isaac	(A)
Marshall, Josiah	(A)
Martin, Enoch	(BCD)
Mason and Lathrop, Messrs.	(C)

Mason, Rev. Charles	(D)
Mason, J.	(C)
Mason, Jonathan	(A)
Mason, Robert M.	(CD)
Mason, William P.	(AD)
Massachusetts Agricultural Society	(A)
May, Samuel	(A)
Mayo, John M.	(D)
McKean, Joseph W. *M.D.*	(AB)
Merriam, Charles	(D)
Merrill, Amos B.	(CD)
Miles, Solomon P.	(AB)
Mills, James K.	(CD)
Minot, William	(CD)
Mixter, Charles	(D)
Moody, David	(A)
Moody, D. F.	(A)
Moody, Paul	(A)
Motley, Thomas	(ABCD)
Mott, Rev. M. J.	(B)
Motte, Rev. J. M.	(B)
Motte, Rev. Mellish	(A)
Munson, Israel	(A)

N

Neale, Rev. R. H.	(B)
Nichols, Benjamin R.	(ABCD)
Norton, Charles E.	(D)

O

O'Brien, Carolan	(D)
Odin, John	(A)
Oliver, F. J.	(A)
Oliver, Nathan *M.D.*	(B)
Osgood, David *M.D.*	(ABCD)
Otis, Arthur H.	(D)
Otis, George W. *M.D.*	(AB)
Otis, H. G.	(ABC)

P

Page, Henry A.	(CD)
Paige, James W.	(D)
Paige, T. H.	(A)
Paine, F. W.	(A)
Palfrey, Rev. J. G.	(BC)
Parker, Charles Hamilton	(CD)
Parker, Charles Henry	(D)
Parker, Daniel P.	(ABCD)
Parker, Francis E.	(CD)
Parker, George S.	(C)
Parker, Henry T.	(C)
Parker, Isaac	(A)
Parker, James	(D)
Parker, John	(B)
Parker, John Jr.	(A)

Parker, Peter	(AB)
Parker, Rev. Theodore	(CD)
Parker, William A.	(D)
Parkman, Charles	(BC)
Parkman, Daniel	(A)
Parkman, Rev. Francis *D.D.*	(ABCD)
Parkman, Francis Jr.	(D)
Parkman, George *M.D.*	(AB)
Parkman, George F.	(CD)
Parkman, John	(A)
Parkman, Rev. John	(D)
Parkman, Samuel *M.D.*	(CD)
Parks, W. S.	(D)
Parris, Alexander	(AB)
Parrott, William P.	(CD)
Parsons, Theophilus	(ABCD)
Parsons, Thomas W. Jr. *M.D.*	(CD)
Parsons, Thomas W.	(B)
Parsons, William	(ABD)
Payne, E. W.	(A)
Payne, William Edward	(A)
Payson, Arthur L.	(C)
Peabody, Rev. Ephraim	(BCD)
Pelham, Charles	(B)
Perkins, James	(A)
Perkins, Mrs. James	(AB)
Perkins, Stephen H.	(ABCD)
Perkins, Hon. Thomas H.	(ABCD)
Perkins, Thomas H. Jr.	(D)
Perkins, William P.	(AB)
Phelps, Rev. Austin	(BC)
Phillips, Edw.	(A)
Phillips, Jonathan	(ABCD)
Phillips, Stephen H.	(CD)
Phipps, Samuel	(CD)
Pickering, Octavius	(ABD)
Pickman, William	(A)
Pierce, John	(A)
Pirscher, Mr.	(A)
Pope, Thomas B.	(B)
Porter, Eliphalet	(A)
Porter, Jonathan	(ABCD)
Pratt, George	(CD)
Pratt, William	(AB)
Prescott, William	(A)
Prescott, William H. *LL.D.*	(ABCD)
Prince, John Jr.	(A)
Putnam, B. W.	(D)
Putnam, C. G. *M.D.*	(C)
Putnam, Jesse	(AB)
Putnam, Oliver	(A)
Putnam, Samuel R.	(BCD)

Q

Quincy, Edmund	(BCD)
Quincy, Hon. Josiah	(ABCD)
Quincy, Hon. Josiah Jr.	(ABCD)

R

Rand, Edward S. (of Newburyport)	(B)
Randall, Mrs. Elizabeth	(CD)
Randall, John *M.D.*	(AB)
Read, William *M.D.*	(CD)
Reed, Benjamin	(A)
Reed, Sampson	(CD)
Reilly, Devin	(D)
Revere, Joseph W.	(ACD)
Reynolds, Edward Jr.	(AB)
Reynolds, Grindall	(D)
Rice, Henry	(AB)
Rice, Henry A.	(D)
Rice, Henry G.	(ABCD)
Rice, T. P.	(A)
Rich, Samuel H.	(AB)
Richards, Fr.	(A)
Richards, John Jr.	(A)
Richards, Reuben	(AB)
Richardson, Albert L.	(D)
Richardson, Jeffrey	(A)
Richardson, Jesse	(AB)
Richardson, William	(C)
Ripley, Rev. George	(AB)
Robbins, Rev. Chandler	(ABCD)
Robbins, Edward H.	(ACD)
Robbins, James M.	(BCD)
Robinson, Rev. Prof. E. (of Andover)	(AB)
Robinson, Horatio	(A)
Rogers, Henry B.	(ABCD)
Rogers, Henry D.	(CD)
Rogers, Rev. William M.	(BCD)
Rogerson, Robert	(A)
Rollins, Mrs. E.	(CD)
Rollins, Ebenezer	(AB)
Ropes, William	(AD)
Rotch, B. S.	(C)
Russell, Benjamin	(A)
Russell, Le Baron *M.D.*	(C)
Russell, Samuel H.	(CD)
Ruthvern, Mrs. Helen	(A)

S

Salisbury, Edward E.	(A)
Salisbury, Josiah Sr.	(A)
Salisbury, Samuel	(AB)
Salter, Richard H. *M.D.*	(D)
Sanger, George P.	(D)
Sargent, Howard	(A)

Sargent, Ignatius	(CD)
Sargent, Lucius Manlius	(CD)
Savage, James	(ACD)
Sawyer, Thomas	(A)
Sawyer, William	(AB)
Sayles, Mrs. Maria F.	(CD)
Sayles, Willard	(C)
Scholfield, Arthur	(BCD)
Searl, George	(A)
Searle, George W.	(D)
Sears, David	(ACD)
Seaver, Benjamin	(CD)
Shackford, Rev. Charles C.	(BCD)
Shattuck, George C.	(ABCD)
Shattuck, George C. Jr. M.D.	(C)
Shattuck, Lemuel	(BCD)
Shaw, Charles B.	(CD)
Shaw, Lemuel	(CD)
Shaw, Robert G.	(ABCD)
Shaw, Robert G. Jr.	(D)
Sheafe, Charles C.	(D)
Shelton, Philo S.	(D)
Shepherd, R. D.	(A)
Sherwin, Thomas	(AB)
Shimmin, Charles F.	(CD)
Shurtleff, Samuel A.	(ABC)
Sigourney, Henry	(ABCD)
Simpson, M. H.	(C)
Skilton, James	(D)
Skinner, Francis	(BCD)
Smith, Rev. Amos	(BC)
Smith, Charles C.	(D)
Smith, Henry W.	(D)
Smith, Isaac	(A)
Smith, James W.	(CD)
Snelling, G. H.	(A)
Sohier, William D.	(CD)
Sprague, Charles	(CD)
Stackpole, J. L.	(BC)
Stanton, Francis	(AB)
Stanwood, Lemuel	(CD)
Starbuck, C. C.	(A)
Stearns, John	(CD)
Stevenson, J. G.	(A)
Stickney, John	(A)
Stimson, Caleb M.	(AD)
Stone, Henry O.	(BCD)
Stone, William W.	(CD)
Storer, D. H. M.D.	(BCD)
Storrow, Charles S.	(D)
Story, Mrs.	(CD)
Story, Franklin H. Jr.	(CD)
Story, W. W.	(C)
Strong, Woodbridge M.D.	(ABCD)
Stuart, Gilbert	(A)
Sturgis, R. L.	(B)
Sturgis, Russell	(A)

Sturgis, William	(ABCD)
Sullivan, Hon. Richard	(ABC)
Sullivan, William	(AB)
Sumner, Charles	(BCD)
Swett, Elizabeth B.	(D)
Swett, Samuel	(ABCD)

T

Tappan, Charles	(A)
Tappan, John	(ABCD)
Tappan, Lewis	(A)
Taylor, Charles	(AB)
Teft, Rev. B. F.	(B)
Thacher, Charles	(CD)
Thacher, P. O.	(A)
Thayer, Andrew E.	(CD)
Thayer, John E.	(B)
Thomas, Dr. Alexander	(B)
Thomas, Isaiah	(A)
Thorndike, Augustus	(A)
Thorndike, Charles	(A)
Thorndike, Israel	(AB)
Thorndike, Israel Jr.	(A)
Ticknor, George	(ABCD)
Tidd, Jacob	(A)
Tilden, Joseph	(ABCD)
Timmins, Henry	(CD)
Torrey, Charles	(ABCD)
Torrey, Samuel	(ABCD)
Towne, Rev. Joseph H.	(BC)
Townsend, S. D. M.D.	(ABCD)
Treadwell, Daniel	(AB)
Tucker, R. D.	(A)
Tuckerman, Edward	(A)
Tuckerman, Edward Jr.	(B)
Tuckerman, Gustavus	(B)
Tuckerman, Henry H.	(AB)
Tuckerman, Rev. Joseph D.D.	(AB)
Tudor, William	(A)

U

Upham, J. B. M.D.	(CD)
Upton, George B.	(D)

W

Wainwright, Rev. D. D. D.D.	(A)
Wainwright, Rev. Jonathan M.	(B)
Waldo, Henry Sidney	(D)
Waldo, Henry S. Jr.	(C)
Waldron, Samuel W.	(B)
Wales, Thomas B.	(ABC)
Walker, Charles	(A)

Walker, W. J.	(A)	Whitney, Moses	(B)
Walley, S. H.	(A)	Whitney, Moses Jr.	(A)
Ward, Thomas W. Esq.	(ABCD)	Whitney, Warren J.	(B)
Ware, Charles E. *M.D.*	(D)	Whitney, William F.	(CD)
Ware, John *M.D.*	(ABCD)	Whitwell, Samuel Jr.	(A)
Warren, Hon. Charles H.	(CD)	Wigglesworth, Edward	(ABCD)
Warren, Edward *M.D.*	(ABCD)	Wigglesworth, Thomas	(ABCD)
Warren, George W.	(B)	Wild, Charles *M.D.*	(AB)
Warren, John C. *M.D.*	(CD)	Willard, Sidney	(A)
Warren, J. Mason *M.D.*	(CD)	Willard, Solomon	(AB)
Warren, J. W. *M.D.*	(B)	Williams, Henry W. *M.D.*	(D)
Warren, John C. *M.D.*	(AB)	Williams, John	(A)
Waterbury, Rev. J. B.		Williams, John D.	(AC)
D.D.	(C)	Williams, Moses	(CD)
Waterson, Robert	(AB)	Williams, Samuel K.	(C)
Watson, Rev. John Lee	(B)	Williams, Thomas	(A)
Webb, Seth Jr.	(D)	Williams, Timothy	(AB)
Webster, Daniel	(A)	Willis, Benjamin	(AB)
Webster, Fletcher	(CD)	Winchester, Amasa	(A)
Welch, John H.	(D)	Winchester, Edmund	(A)
Welles, Arnold	(B)	Wing, Benjamin F. *M.D.*	(CD)
Welles, Benjamin	(AB)	Winslow, Isaac	(ABCD)
Welles, John	(A)	Winthrop, Thomas L.	(A)
Welles, William Jr.	(A)	Wolcott, J. H.	(CD)
Wells, William Jr.	(B)	Wormeley, R. R.	(A)
Weston, Alden B.	(ABCD)	Wright, H. H.	(B)
Wheelwright, William W.	(A)	Wright, Dr. John H.	(C)
Whipple, Charles K.	(CD)	Wyman, Jeffers *M.D.*	(CD)
Whipple, Edwin P.	(CD)	Wyman, Rufus	(AB)
Whipple, John A.	(D)		
White, William O.	(D)		
Whiting, Nathaniel	(CD)	**Y**	
Whiting, William	(D)		
Whitmore, C. J.	(D)	Young, A. B.	(B)
Whitney, Benjamin D.	(ABCD)	Young, Rev. Alexander	(AB)
Whitney, Joseph	(CD)	Young, Edward J.	(CD)

GUESTS WHOM EMERSON INTRODUCED TO THE BOSTON ATHENÆUM*

Date	Guest	Residence	Vol. and page
1823, [Dec. 30]	Oliver H. Blood	Stirling, Mass.	I, ...
1827, Aug. 19	M. I. Motte	Charleston, S. C.	I, ...
1829, Aug. 20	Joseph Todhunter	Philadelphia	II, ...
1829, [Dec. 16]	William A. Kent	Concord, N. H.	II, ...
1831, July 24 {	William Emerson	New York	
	Samuel Bradford	Philadelphia	II, ...
1832, [Feb. 1]	Warren Burton	Wilton, N. H.	II, ...
1832, Aug. 24	E. B. Emerson	Porto Rico	II, ...
1833, Oct. 16	Thomas Davis	Virginia	II, ...
1841, Dec. 3	Henry D. Thoreau	Concord, Mass.	II, ...
1843, Jan. 3	H. G. Wright	London	II, ...
1849, Nov. 1	Henry James	New York	III, 12
1850, July 18	J. E. Goodson	Cincinnati	III, 39
1856, [Dec. 22]	Daniel Ricketson	New Bedford	III, 189
1857, [Oct. 12]	George S. Phillips	Leeds, England	III, 197
1858, [Dec. 1]	Thomas Cholmondeley	London	III, 205
1859, [Feb. 24]	Fitz-James O'Brien	New York	III, 208
1860, [Mar. 17]	W. Whitman	Brooklyn, N. Y.	III, 215
1861, Jan. 26	Nath[anie]l Hawthorne Esq.	Concord	III, 219
1863, Feb. 28	A. A. Manning [?Canning]	Brooklyn, N. Y.	III, 232

*Among the valuable records of the Athenæum are four volumes bearing the title, *Names of Strangers Introduced*, (B.A. W 1815-1883), containing a record from 1815 to 1883 of the distinguished guests who visited the library and art gallery, with their signatures and the signatures of their sponsors. One might say, truthfully, that these books are a record of the celebrities who visited Boston from all parts of the United States and Europe during that period. [Vol. I (1815-1827); vol. II (1828-1848); vol. III (1849-1865); vol. IV (1865-1883)] When no date is given opposite a signature in the records, I have supplied in brackets the next preceding date.

Date	Guest	Residence	Vol. and page
1863, [Aug. 15]	Rich[ard] Randolph Jr.	Philadelphia	III, 233
1863,　Aug. 29	W. H. Furness Jr.	Germantown, Phila.	III, 234
1863, [Nov. 21]	Philip P. Randolph	Philadelphia	III, 234
1865,　May　4	William Emerson	Concord	IV,　4
1865,　Aug. 25	F. Willson	Cambridge	IV,　6
1865,　Sept. 18	Joseph Albree	Pittsburgh, Pa.	IV.　6
1867, [May 21]	William G. Bryan	Batavia, N. Y.	IV,　15
1868, [Feb. 26]	Rev. S. Phillips Day	London, England	IV,　17
1868, [June 16]	Franklin Taylor	Westchester, Pa.	IV,　19
1869, [Mar. 16]	Justin McCarthy	London, England	IV,　27

BOOKS WHICH EMERSON ASKED THE ATHENÆUM
TO SECURE FOR HIS USE*

1848, Nov. 23	Camden's *Britannia* (Holland's Translation)	I,	156
1849, Feb. 19	Robert Browning's *Poetical Works*		
	[Requested by D. S. Gilchrist also.]	I,	158
1854, [Mar. 8]	*London Leader*	I,	190
1855, [Apr. 14]	*Des Pensées de Pascal* (Victor Cousin's edition,		
	1843)	I,	206
1855, Sept. 4	*Life of Dr. Abernethy* (reprinted New York)	I,	212
1856, Aug. [ ]	*The Works* of Horace Binney Wallace	I,	234
1857, Mar. 12	Richard Gray, *Memòria Technica* (new ed.),		
	London, 1851	II,	10
1857, May 1	Arago, *Lives of Distinguished Scientific Men*		
	translated by Baden Powell	II,	14
1857, May 1	Arago, *Autobiography* (tr. Baden Powell)	II,	14
1857, May 1	W. S. Landor, *Works*, London, 1852 (2 vols.)	II,	14
1857, May 1	W. S. Landor, *Last Fruits of an Old Tree*	II,	14
1857, May 1	Plutarch's *Morals* (English Translation)		
	London, 1718 (5 vols.)	II,	16
1857, May 1	Thomas Taylor, *Select Works of Plotinus* (1 vol.)	II,	16
1857, May 1	Thomas Taylor, *Iamblichus' Life of Pythagoras*	II,	16
1857, May 1	Thomas Taylor, *Iamblichus on the Mysteries,*		
	London, 1821	II,	16
1857, May 1	Thomas Taylor, *Proclus, Commentaries on the*		
	Timæus of Plato, London, 1816 (2 vols.)	II,	16
1857, May 1	Thomas Taylor, *Select Works of Porphyry,*		
	London, 1823	II,	16

----

*In a set of volumes entitled, *Books Asked For* (B.A. Wre) : vol. I (1826-1857) ; vol. II (1857-1865) ; vol. III (1865-1870), vol. IV (1870-1873). When no date appears opposite a listing in these volumes, I have supplied in brackets the next preceding date.

1857, May 1   *Upanishads* [vol. XV of *Bibliotheca Indica*, published under patronage of the Directors of the East India Co.] Tr. from Sanscrit by D. E. Roer, Calcutta, 1853   II, 16

1857, May 1   Lady Charlotte Guest, *The Mabinogion* from the Llyfr Còch o Hergest, and other ancient Welsh Mss., London, 1839 etc.   II, 16

1863, [Feb. 9]   Ernest Renan, *Histoire et Système comparé des Langues Sémitiques* / and his latest brochures   II, 242

1867, [May 28]   *Life of Lessing*, by Stahr; tr. by Evans   III, 102

1871, [Nov. 20]   *Popular Ballads and Songs*, ed. Robert Jamieson, Edinburgh, 1806   (2 vols.)   IV, 116